LINGUISTICS IN THE COURTROOM

LINGUISTICS IN THE COURTROOM
A Practical Guide

Roger W. Shuy

OXFORD
UNIVERSITY PRESS

2006

OXFORD
UNIVERSITY PRESS

Oxford University Press, Inc., publishes works that further
Oxford University's objective of excellence
in research, scholarship, and education.

Oxford   New York
Auckland   Cape Town   Dar es Salaam   Hong Kong   Karachi
Kuala Lumpur   Madrid   Melbourne   Mexico City   Nairobi
New Delhi   Shanghai   Taipei   Toronto

With offices in
Argentina   Austria   Brazil   Chile   Czech Republic   France   Greece
Guatemala   Hungary   Italy   Japan   Poland   Portugal   Singapore
South Korea   Switzerland   Thailand   Turkey   Ukraine   Vietnam

Published by Oxford University Press, Inc.
198 Madison Avenue, New York, New York 10016

www.oup.com

Oxford is a registered trademark of Oxford University Press

Library of Congress Cataloging-in-Publication Data
Shuy, Roger W.
Linguistics in the courtroom: a practical guide / Roger W. Shuy.
   p. cm
Includes bibliographical references and index.
ISBN-13 978-0-19-530664-4

1. Forensic linguistics—United States.   I. Title.
KF8968.54S483 2006
347.73'67—dc22   2005040185

Printed in the United States of America
on acid-free paper

Preface

As more linguists are being asked to consult with lawyers and testify at trials, there is a need for a nuts-and-bolts guidebook on how to be a forensic linguist. This book is written both for newer scholars who plan to do this work and for established linguists who haven't done work like this before but who are suddenly called on to do so. Based on my thirty years of experience, this book deals with issues of how to become an expert, how to start a practice of consulting on law cases, how to manage a consulting business, how to work with attorneys, how to write reports and affidavits, and how to participate successfully in depositions, direct examination, and cross-examination at trial. Finally the book also suggests ways that linguists can use their forensic linguistic experiences in their publications and classroom teaching, along with suggestions of recent helpful books forensic linguists may need for their personal libraries.

Although I focus on the U.S. law arena, I also include some of the slightly different practices between the United States and the United Kingdom. In U.S. civil cases, for example, it is common for experts to be deposed before testifying at trial. The deposition (see chapter 7), as it occurs in the United States, is relatively unknown in most of the United Kingdom, where instead it is common for the expert's written report or affidavit (see chapter 6) to be made available to the opposing side well in advance. There is a provision in Scottish law for a procedure called *precognition* whereby a representative for one side may visit witnesses and interview them about what they will say.

In the United States, almost invariably experts are hired by lawyers representing the opposing parties in law cases, whereas in many other countries the experts are engaged by the court to provide their knowledge and analysis to the judge. Some U.S. experts would prefer the European system, because it seems to avoid some of the problems related to impressions of bias or advocacy with which U.S. experts are sometimes saddled. Also very rare in the United States is the occasional practice in the United Kingdom when judges request opposing experts to get together and produce an agreed-on statement.

The procedures for determining whether an expert is admissible as an expert are also a bit different between the United Kingdom and America. In England and Australia, for example, only the qualification of the expert is assessed. In the United States admissibility depends not only on the expert's qualifications but also on the methods used in the expert's analysis (see chapter 8). I am told, however, that the U.S. *Daubert* and *Kumho* decisions (see chapter 8) are being discussed in the United Kingdom and are likely to cross the ocean in one way or another at some time.

The focus of this book is on ways that linguists can learn to work with lawyers. The base field for such an alliance— the place where the activity is located, the place where the rubber hits the road—is law. The contributing field is linguistics. This is not to say that linguistics isn't able to help change the field of law, but that is not the goal I'm talking about here. It's not what most trial lawyers are asking of us, and they may think linguists a bit arrogant to think that we can help change the processes of law. Their immediate need is for help with their cases in places where language issues are central.

FOR LINGUISTICS STUDENTS

I often receive requests from young scholars who tell me that they want to become forensic linguists. Among other things, many ask for advice about where they can go to study forensic linguistics. At the risk of sounding radical, let me explain that I don't think we need to add yet another subfield to the already burgeoning college curriculum. Even if an academic major in forensic linguistics were created, I'm not sure that we know what it should contain. Linguistics departments already teach linguistics. Law schools already teach law.

Do linguists really need to learn law in order to do a linguistic analysis of legal documents, and do lawyers really need to learn linguistics in order to be successful in their cases? I think not. It would seem more efficient for both fields to learn how to work with each other. On the other hand, there are some things that both fields need to know about each other to be able to work well together.

At the time of this writing, a small number of programs called forensic linguistics currently exist. I can't evaluate them, but I would hope that the teaching of linguistics is primary in such programs and that their focus on forensic linguistics is treated as a way of applying the tools of linguistics to the particular legal issues that relate to language. Similarly, I can also visualize law degree programs that teach courses in the ways that linguistic analysis might help in preparing law students for the legal profession, although I have yet not heard of any such programs.

In the United States there are a few universities that offer courses in forensic linguistics (sometimes called linguistics and law), but as far as I know, few academic degrees are offered in this subject. I am not convinced that there is a need for such a major. First and foremost, you need to be a linguist to use this field to deal with the data provided by law cases. I know some of the linguists who teach courses called forensic linguistics, and I have high regard for them. But I and a number of others in the field have come to doubt whether entire programs in forensic linguistics are really necessary.

So my general advice to the young scholars who contact me goes like this. For forensic linguists to be considered an expert witness in law cases, they are required to go through three developmental stages:

Stage 1. Becoming a linguist.

Stage 2. Becoming an expert in linguistics.

Stage 3. Learning how to work and testify as a linguistics expert.

Chapter 1 of this book addresses the first two of these stages, the stages of development that have to be accomplished before a person can be called on as an expert in linguistics in the most useful and effective manner.

FOR ESTABLISHED LINGUISTS

I also get queries from established linguists about how to deal with requests from attorneys to help them with their law cases. The rest of the book addresses the needs of established linguists (stage 3) covering most of the nuts and bolts of working with attorneys and testifying at trials. As this book is being written, more and more linguists are beginning to make themselves available as experts in law cases, and many of them are doing this for the first time. This book is intended to help pave the road for them as they make an effective journey in this field.

The organization of this book more or less follows the sequence of events that take place from the time an expert is called by an attorney to the completion of testimony at trial.

The sequence can be aborted at any time, of course, but if things go well, there are fifteen steps in the process:

1. The lawyer calls the expert for help on a case.
2. The expert sends a CV and a record of relevant court experience to the lawyer.
3. The work agreement is negotiated—rates, letters of agreement, confidentiality agreement, schedules.
4. The lawyer sends the materials to the expert.
5. The expert decides whether to work on the case.
6. If the expert agrees to work on it, the data are analyzed.
7. The expert orally reports preliminary findings to the lawyer.
8. The expert prepares a written report or affidavit (in civil cases).
9. The expert is deposed by the opposing lawyer (in civil cases).
10. The expert reports for trial.
11. An offer of proof is made to the court.
12. The expert begins testimony with qualifications, followed by voir dire by the opposing lawyer.
13. The expert gives direct testimony.
14. The expert is cross-examined by the opposing lawyer.
15. Redirect and recross may take place.

Not all of these steps need to occur. For example, written reports are not frequently required in criminal cases, and in most criminal cases the expert is not deposed. Most civil cases are settled long before trial takes place, and most criminal cases are settled with plea bargains of various types. I have worked on some 500 cases over the years, only about 10 percent of which ever called me to testify. Pretrial settlements and plea agreements do not mean that the work done by the expert is in vain. In many cases, the products of expert analysis lead directly to such settlements and plea bargains.

Contents

LINGUISTICS IN THE COURTROOM

First Steps

As OBVIOUS AS THIS MAY SOUND, SOMEHOW THE FACT that one first has to become a linguist seems to get lost on some aspiring forensic linguists. There's no need to try to apply linguistics to any other area of life before you've first learned what it is that you have to apply.

ON DEFINING FORENSIC LINGUISTICS

It may be useful here to comment on the term *forensic linguistics*. It has become a useful way to refer to the use of linguistics knowledge in law cases where there are data that serve as evidence. But I have some concerns about the term itself, because it seems to me that when one does "forensic linguistics" one is simply doing linguistics, a type of applied linguistics, in fact. In an age of ever increasing specializations, I suppose it only natural that applied linguistics would spawn further subspecialties, such as "educational linguistics," "language learning," "language assessment," and (hopefully not)

3

"medical linguistics." Currently, "forensic linguistics" is being used to describe this subfield.

One problem with the increase of specializations is that participants in such areas tend to isolate themselves from the discipline that feeds them. Such isolation includes a dangerous tendency that can cause participants to neglect the foundations on which the subspecialties are built. For this reason, whenever I am called to the witness stand and am asked to describe my field of expertise, I reply that it is linguistics. If the questioner asks if I'm a forensic linguist, I respond that this is a term used by some people these days but that I prefer to call what I do "applied linguistics." Despite my qualms about the term, in recent years *forensic linguistics* has come to describe this work and, right or wrong, I am slowly beginning to accept that this is a convenient way for lawyers and linguists alike to talk about this area. But mere convenience is no excuse for letting it become isolated from its roots.

My fervent hope is that the "linguistics" part of the term will be preserved and not be misused to include such areas of expertise currently called document analysis, handwriting analysis, type-token analysis, or statement analysis, which come closer to a content analysis of words or word parts. Certain types of stylistic analysis also might be excluded. Simply counting language features is not the same as linguistic analysis.

Although it is reasonably clear what the tools of linguistics are, it is useful to remember and reflect what they mean when one thinks about forensic linguistics. Any proficient worker has a tool kit from which the correct tools are selected to analyze specific written or spoken texts. The following list describes the basic tool kit needed by a forensic linguist, accompanied here by only the briefest of examples relevant to the context of linguistics and law (okay, I'll say it—to the context of forensic linguistics).

1. Phonetics and Phonology

Many training programs in linguistics stress phonology, the systematic use of sounds, which is well and good, but sometimes the study of phonetics, the sounds themselves, is overlooked. It's a remnant of the previous era of descriptive linguistics, when phonetic skills were learned to transcribe new languages. The more that linguistics turned to abstract and philosophical concerns about language (by no means a bad thing), the more some of the earlier linguistic tools seemed to be abandoned.

In many law cases where linguists are called on, skills in phonetics are needed. Trademark cases, where issues of potential consumer confusion abound, easily come to mind. Do the product names Health Selections and Healthy Choice sound enough alike to cause confusion? Is Mead Data Central's Lexis pronounced the same as Toyota's Lexus? The linguist should not be asked to opine about how the public pronounces these (unless research from surveys indicate otherwise), but their job is to point out the sameness or difference in the sounds used, or potentially used, in such names, leaving the ultimate opinion to the judge or jury. Skills in phonetics are a necessity for this.

2. Morphology

Knowledge of the meaning units that make up words in any language is central in many types of law cases. It can help identify such things as:

- dialect differences in speaker identification cases,
- whether an alleged illegal act was completed or spoken of hypothetically, and
- distinguishing aspects of differences in trademark names.

Even the variations found in meanings conveyed by morphemes have been important in law cases.

3. Syntax

The way sentences are constructed plays an essential role in such areas as authorship identification and contract disputes, to mention only two. The grammatical scope of a noun phrase may be the focus of differences between opposing party's conflicting understandings of a contract. Although authorship identification cases may seem to be about spelling, punctuation, and grammatical errors, it is generally believed that syntactic usage works better to make such identification, because syntax operates at the least conscious level of a writer or speaker.

4. Semantics

Meaning is at the core of most civil and criminal cases. The meaning of the prefix, *Mc-*, can be traced from its origins as a patronymic prefix to its current understanding as "inexpensive," "convenient," "mass produced," and "widely available," all produced by McDonald's restaurants. In an insurance contract dispute, the policy's words, "We do not cover property in or on a vehicle that is not attended" opens the door to semantic analysis of *in, vehicle,* and *attended.*

5. Pragmatics

Intention is at the very center of many criminal cases. Although linguistics (or any other field for that matter) cannot with certainty identify intentions, linguistic analysis can reveal clues to intentions that are provided by indirectness, politeness strategies, and other pragmatic functions.

6. Speech Acts

The speech acts of offering, denying, accepting, apologizing, and many others are frequently significant in criminal cases of bribery and sexual misconduct. They also can play an important role in contract disputes, discrimination, and copyright infringement cases.

7. Language Variation and Change

Knowledge of dialectology and sociolinguistics can be extremely important in speaker identification cases, among others. The processes of language change are also central in many trademark and contract dispute cases.

8. Discourse Analysis

Much of the evidence in civil and criminal cases involves the use of continuous discourse. In undercover criminal cases, for example, tape-recorded discourse provides virtually all of the evidence. But the discourse structure of contracts and product liability cases can offer every bit as much information as the words used. Careful analysis of topic introduction and recycling, the fronting of main ideas, the use of discourse markers, and other discourse features can be critical.

9. Lexicography

Most linguists are not well trained in lexicography, but trademark and contract dispute cases frequently allow dictionary definitions to be used at trial. Acceptable practices of dictionary production are not widely known outside the field of lexicography but are accessible to linguists if they do a bit of digging.

10. Language Assessment and Testing

Not all linguists get training in this area. Psycholinguists, especially those who work in language development, or other applied linguists with such training tend to be called on to assess the language ability of suspects accused of crimes. For example, can an accused person sufficiently be able to understand and be understood well enough to be held responsible for the contents of a message? Or does the language evidence accurately reflect the speaker's actual "voice"?

In summary, linguists call on the contents of their tool kits to address the data and issues of other fields, such as education, medical communication, negotiation, diplomacy, or advertising. Good applied linguists must know and be able to use the tools of their field. When data situated in real life, such as legal proceedings, are presented for analysis, linguists use those tools to help solve the problem. So first of all, scholars calling themselves forensic linguists need to be professionally trained linguists, preferably with the highest academic degree possible.

BECOMING AN EXPERT

As the field of law seems to see it, an expert is somebody who has not only the credentials of training but also a successful work record beyond that. For academics, that usually means publications and presentations at academic meetings.

A Publication Record

To be considered an expert in anything, one normally needs the best credentials possible. Obtaining a doctorate is one of the best credentials of an expert. But that is only the starting point. To be considered an expert, it's also necessary to build a track record of publications in your field of expertise. Forensic linguists are, for the most part, not only scholars who have graduate degrees in linguistics but those who have also published articles and books in the linguistic areas in which they have specialized, such as syntax, discourse analysis, pragmatics, speech acts, semantics, psycholinguistics, discourse analysis, or sociolinguistics. Without such a track record, it can become awkward when they are cross-examined by attorneys or other opponents who can and will challenge their expertise.

For example, in the recent International Tribunal on Rwanda, the prosecution used an expert witness who claimed to have called on his expert knowledge of sociolinguistics to show that a certain Rwandan newspaper editor had written articles that incited genocide. My review of his report and testimony showed clearly that he knew very little about sociolinguistics, because his analysis had practically nothing to do with sociolinguistics. When he did claim to be calling on such knowledge, it was usually misguided. The defense attorney asked me to rebut and therefore impeach this man's report and trial testimony, which was relatively simple to do. A check of his academic background showed that he had only one introductory course in sociolinguistics in his doctoral program at a British university. He had not achieved expert status in the field he claimed.

Do We Need to Be Trained in Law?

In some areas, such as psycholinguistics, it may be necessary for the linguist to know a good bit about another field of study, psychology in this case. In other areas that move across disciplinary boundaries, this need may not be as strong. It's my opinion, for example, that expert witnesses in forensic linguistics do not need to also become experts in law. I have always felt that my work analyzing language in civil and criminal cases is independent of what the law says. Legal knowledge is the province of the attorney with whom I'm working. The language is the language, regardless of how the law views it.

On the other hand, some linguists gain distinct advantages by being experts with degrees in both linguistics and law. The two fields can be mutually nurturing, leading those with expertise in both fields to produce analyses that those with only one field of expertise may not be able to do nearly as well. But having a law degree can sometimes also limit them from participating in some areas that seem to be more common only for linguists without legal training, namely, in being an expert witness. I've recommended several such linguist/lawyers over and over again to attorneys who call me, and their response is usually, "I don't need another lawyer." I'm not sure what this means, but one thing I know is that they wanted a linguist as an expert. Despite my personal innocence of formal legal training, in some of my affidavits and reports in civil cases, opposition lawyers have accused me of making legal arguments, an apparent no-no unless one is an attorney. It's hard to understand such accusations because I wouldn't know a legal argument when I saw one.

Training in law certainly helps linguists who work on matters of legal language (Tiersma 1999), drafting jury instructions (Charrow and Charrow 1979), and other matters. These linguistically based contributions are indeed important, and more work of this type should be encouraged. The average linguist without a law degree may not be able to do this type of analysis, and such work may not have the impact that it could have without being part of the legal fraternity. So the decision about whether a linguist should get legal training cuts two ways, depending the type of relationship one wants to have with the legal community.

REFERENCES

Charrow, Veda R., and Robert P. Charrow. 1979. "Making Legal Language Understandable: A Psycholinguistic Study of Jury Instructions." Columbia Law Review 79 (7): 1306–74.

2

Starting a Practice

ONCE YOU HAVE BECOME A LINGUIST AND YOU'VE PUB-
lished enough in your field to be considered an expert, you
may sit by your telephone or scroll the inbox of your e-mail
looking for invitations to flow in from attorneys. Sorry, it
just doesn't happen that way. Even the few attorneys out
there who happen to know what a linguist is probably won't
know who you are. And they might not know how to find
you if they did. If they do happen to stumble onto you, they
will want to know about your experience in this field. One
of the first questions asked of me early in my work was,
"Have you ever testified at trial?" For a beginner, this question can end the interview. The lawyer needs somebody who
has been there before.

Fortunately for me, the first case I ever worked on was a
high-profile solicitation to murder case in Texas. I was equally
fortunate to have testified in that trial. I was still more fortunate that my testimony was publicly claimed to have been
critical in the jury's decision to acquit the defendant. Word
of this event spread quickly among defense attorneys not only

in Texas but also across the country. My phone began ring-
ing from the start.

But my case was unusual. So when linguists ask me how
they can get started, here is what I tell them.

CONSTRUCTING A SPECIALIZED CURRICULUM VITAE

One of your best promotional devices is a clear and readable
record of your qualifications and experience. All linguists
know that the CV is important for getting an academic job.
But the task here is to attract consulting work on a law case,
not a job teaching phonology or pragmatics. So you recast
your CV slightly to suit the audience. Just like your regular
CV, it should include all your degrees and the universities
where you earned them. It should include your academic
standing and titles and, of course, a record of your publications and important academic presentations. But it is particularly helpful if you can categorize your publications in ways
that attract the interest of attorneys. For example, instead
of just listing only their arcane titles, arrange them under
headings such as "Identification of Word Meanings," which
suggests to linguistically naive lawyers that you might be able
to help them with trademark cases involving the meanings
associated with trade names. Because the word *semantics*
carries unfortunate baggage in the courts and with the general public, it may be prudent to avoid using that term as a
heading. If you have a category called "Phonology," you

might think about captioning it with a title such as "Speech Sounds," which might resonate better with an attorney looking for a linguist to help identify or exclude a tape recording of his client in a narcotics case.

ADVERTISING

A few linguists that I've heard of, apparently more eager than most to attract consultantships, advertise their availability commercially in legal journals, such as *The National Law Review* or the *Legal Times.* Apparently this tactic has worked for some of them, because their ads ran for many months. But there is a distinct downside to advertising commercially. In one case I worked on, the opposing side hired a linguist who had advertised in the *Legal Times.* The attorney on my side used this advertising to paint him as a hired gun for anybody who would hire him.

The written or unwritten rules about professionals advertising their wares or services are not exactly clear. Physicians do not normally advertise. Lawyers who advertise may be looked down on by their peers as ambulance chasers. Exactly where linguists fit is still up for grabs, but from my experience at least, commercially advertising one's availability may not set very well in the linguistic community. I have yet to hear a forensic linguistics presentation made by one of the people who advertise this way, and I have not seen any of their forensic linguistic articles published in respectable academic journals. That may tell us something.

In short, the act of commercially advertising one's availability can cause more problems than it's worth. Because we have no clear record that advertising actually works well, and we do have evidence that it pulls the linguist down to the same level as others who advertise commercially, such as handwriting specialists and document analysts, it doesn't seem to be a very promising way to develop one's professional practice.

Rather than commercially advertising your availability, the best advertisement is to become known by lawyers. Criminal lawyers, in particular, talk with each other about their cases. In my experience, civil lawyers don't do this quite as much. In an effort to find out how lawyers learned about me, I have made it a practice to ask attorneys who call me where they got my name. Sometimes it's from books or articles that I've written. More often it's from other lawyers who have used my services or the services of other linguists. More recently I've been told that they found me through Google, which led them to my Web site. I suppose a Web site is in itself a form of advertising, but for me it's a convenient way to avoid having to send attorneys my CV and case experience by mail.

There are many other ways to become known to attorneys. One way is to speak at local or national law conferences about cases you've worked on. Unfortunately, speakers at such meetings are usually invited. So it is wise to get to know some local attorneys. Another way is to have a Web site that makes the words *forensic linguistics* prominent enough to capture the searcher's attention. Some lawyers who look for a linguist will call the nearest university. It can be useful to let your department receptionist know that you are the one to take such calls.

VOLUNTEERING YOUR SERVICES

Even though you may be a qualified linguist and are considered to have expertise in your area of specialization, the door to forensic opportunity may still not open easily. And it's less likely to open without first having some experience under your belt. It's the classic dilemma of looking for a job and being told that you first need to have some experience.

One way to get experience is to volunteer your services to a nearby legal clinic that serves low-income or handicapped citizens. Many law schools have such clinics, and of course there are also national organizations, such as the National Senior Citizens Law Center, and various regional or local service organizations that deal with immigration, bilingualism, minorities, Medicare claims, and other legal matters. Such groups have constantly recurring legal problems to deal with, many of which involve language issues of one type or another. My book *Bureaucratic Language in Government and Business* (1998) describes ways to work with such groups. These organizations may not at first realize that they have issues for linguists to address, as obvious as they may be to you. So a selling job is probably necessary. Be alert to such issues in the local newspaper and follow up with volunteering your assistance. It's not a way to earn a big income, but it can help get you started on such a path, because it can provide you with that needed qualification of experience. It also would be useful to publish articles and give papers about such work as a way of adding to your qualifications as an expert.

FINDING AN ESTABLISHED FORENSIC LINGUIST AS A MENTOR

There may be no better way to gain experience than to become an official or unofficial assistant to a linguist who is already working in this area. If there are professors at your university doing this kind of work, it could be prudent to volunteer to work with them on the next case available. There is always some kind of work that can be done by a newcomer or junior partner. In any case, the mentoring process is often the best way to learn a new form of business. But it's not necessary for the mentor to be at your own university or even within your own geographical region. It's no secret that colleagues within a department are sometimes overly competitive, so the in-house forensic linguist may not be willing to help you become a potential competitor. In such cases, it may be best to find a long-distance mentor. Alliances can be forged at academic meetings, for example, and your best bet for a mentor may well be many miles away. The ease of modern electronic communication makes this much easier than it used to be.

While I was still teaching at Georgetown, I personally hired grad students to assist me with some of the work in my cases. This gave them a source of income as well as valuable experience and insights. Such an arrangement can work well for the professor as well, because the time constraints often involved in forensic work are difficult to meet and we need all the help we can get.

Nor is the mentoring of new forensic linguists limited to grad students. There are several currently established linguists in this field who have consulted me regularly in their early forensic linguistics work. Some still refer to me as their mentor. I would encourage anyone just starting in this field to feel free to check ideas, ask questions, and otherwise get help from more senior forensic linguists, most of whom are eager to help newcomers get started. And I encourage other established linguists to make themselves available to those just starting this work.

DECIDING WHAT KIND OF CASES TO TAKE

Suppose you've volunteered your services and have built some valuable experience. You're now ready to take on a case whenever a lawyer should call you.

Staying within Your Qualifications

One thing to be very careful about is to not take a case for which you are not really qualified. For example, if the case requires knowledge of a certain variety of English and you've had no training in language variation, it's probably not wise to accept it, largely because you will be asked by the opposing lawyer what expertise you have in this area. If you've not studied sociolinguistics or dialectology, it may be wise to pass on this one. Likewise, if your auditory or acoustic phonetics background is weak or nonexistent, it would be prudent to shy away from speaker identification cases.

Checking Your Own Feelings

There is another important area that also should be considered. Some people have emotional discomfort with certain types of crimes, such as child sexual abuse, for example. If working on such cases is troublesome or difficult, it may be wise to avoid them. One prominent Jewish forensic psychologist made it openly clear that she would not take cases that appear to impinge on the rights of Jewish groups or individuals. Another forensic linguist made it clear that he would take criminal cases rather than civil ones because he was more concerned about issues of human justice than about one company making money from another. Some experts are emotionally or ethically unwilling to take on certain types of criminal cases. If the client is accused of murder or rape, the case may be so personally repugnant that they may not want to get involved at all. If you morally object to helping a large corporation win a civil suit against a smaller company, this may suggest a personal reason for staying out of such cases. You have to assess your own feelings at the outset of your work before getting more deeply involved in any particular case. There are good reasons to shun certain types of cases. It is important for lawyers to be informed of such reasons from the beginning. It should not be embarrassing to explain when particular emotional or psychological feelings can block possible efficiency.

3

Doing Business

So the phone finally rings, and the lawyer on the other end
asks you to work on a case. You'll need to take a few precau-
tions before leaping into it. Beware of calls from the clients
themselves, however, because it is always better (and safer)
to work with their attorneys.

Making Sure That It's Doable

Some linguists will not agree to take a case until they are first
given the opportunity to review the data. This is a wise move,
because once the evidence is examined, it may turn out that the
case is not one that is desirable. Once you have agreed to take
a case, it is awkward and embarrassing to back out of it.

Don't Be Pushed

It is wise to pay attention to what the attorneys say when
they first call you. They should describe the nature of their

case, what language data are available, how they got
your name, and what their expectations might be. If the
attorneys are competent, they won't tell you what they
want your analysis to prove. Instead they will ask you
only to examine the evidence from a linguistic perspective. If you agree to take a look at the data, be sure to indicate that even this preliminary look will take some
effort for which you should be compensated. Some experts
charge a flat fee for this initial examination. If they agree,
the lawyers should send you a check along with the case
materials.

Be Sure That You're the Right Expert

One thing to determine is whether your expertise in syntax, discourse analysis, or any other subspecialty is specifically appropriate. You don't want to get boxed in to agreeing
to perform analyses that are outside your expertise. For example, I regularly get calls from attorneys who really
need an acoustic engineer to evaluate whether their tapes
have been altered or tampered with. I keep a list of such
experts in my files, and I simply refer the attorneys to them.
Interestingly, these acoustic engineers also often get calls
for expertise that requires a linguist, and they refer the
attorneys to me for such work. But in most cases when
the attorney makes the appropriate call, the knowledge
that any linguist has of the core areas of our field will
be adequate, even if you didn't write a dissertation in that
specific area.

EXCHANGING INFORMATION

If lawyers who call you appear to be interested in hiring you, they usually ask you send them your curriculum vitae and sometimes a list of any cases you've worked on in the past. In today's world, most of this exchange of information is done electronically. If you already have a Web site containing some of this information, it is easy to refer lawyers to it and let them download whatever they think they need.

CHARGING FOR SERVICES

For many linguists who do this work for the first time, it's hard to think about how much to charge for your services. You may have done some consulting before, but this type of work seems (and is) different. If you plan to do much forensic work, it is prudent to begin to think of this as a business. Lawyers often accept their own cases on a flat-fee basis, but I have never been able to figure out how to do this, so I set an hourly rate and keep a meticulous record of hours, half-hours, and even quarter-hours spent on each case, including analysis time, report writing time, and communication time with the lawyers.

HOW MUCH TO CHARGE

What is this type of work worth? This is hard to say. I don't know what other forensic linguists charge for their services, but in my case I've decided that I should charge as much as a midlevel attorney, especially in most civil cases and in criminal cases where the defendant is well financed. It would seem reasonable to have a single rate for all cases, but the world doesn't seem to work that way. Deep-pocket cases, such as most civil disputes, can command a larger fee than you might be able to charge for many low-budget criminal cases. Therefore I have different fees in my mind when attorneys call. When you take on criminal cases involving court-appointed attorneys, there will likely be an existing negotiated rate for experts. In the United States, each state has its own system, and it's usually necessary to stay within those boundaries, usually from $125 to $150 per hour. The lawyers will explain this more. Government-funded cases in the United Kingdom have set fee scales for experts.

Consulting with government funding tends to be considerably less than what an expert can charge individual attorneys. From what I've been able to determine about the fees of U.S. experts with medical specialties, my own rate tends to be on the relatively low side. Some physicians get $400 or $500 (or even more) per hour, for example. Although I reason that linguistic experts can be worth at least as much, the kind of work we do is usually very different from that of experts in medicine, accounting, or engineering. They don't often need to spend nearly as many hours analyzing data that we do, and although they command a high hourly rate, in the long run the linguist does almost equally well with a lower hourly rate and considerably more hours spent. In any case, the linguistic expert's hourly rate will probably exceed the amount paid by working as a college professor. It is obvious that a newcomer to forensic consulting may want to charge a rate lower than can be commanded once some case experience is under one's belt.

There is also the question of how to charge for trial testimony, as opposed to the time spent in analysis and report writing. Trial testimony usually takes a great deal more out of you than simply sitting at your desk does and therefore deserves a higher rate, something like double the hourly rate for an eight-hour day's work. Most expert witnesses have higher testimony fees than the fees they charge for their analyses. A handy rule of thumb is to charge a flat fee for each day spent at trial, including any part of that day. Much of the expert's time is spent outside the courtroom, waiting to be called to the witness stand. I argue that even if I spend only two hours on the stand at the end of one day and another hour or two on the stand the next day, I am entitled to two full days of payment. This is time taken away from your ability to do other work on such days. I've never been challenged about this.

Of course, all expenses that you incur should be reimbursed, especially travel costs. But what about the time it takes to travel related to the work? This gets a bit tricky. On one hand, the time you spend traveling is time taken away from your other work and therefore travel time seems justified to charge. But not all attorneys and clients see it that way. In such cases I tend to review my analyses and testimony when I fly to the site of the trial. That way I can legitimately charge the hours spent doing this. Whatever you charge, in the United States but not as commonly in the United Kingdom, you can be sure that the opposing attorney will ask you your rate, number of hours spent, and total earnings when he cross-examines you at trial. It is therefore a good idea to be able to be ready to answer such questions completely and honestly. The opposing lawyer's point is to try to get the jury to believe that you are making a lot of money on this case, a lot more than they make in their jobs and certainly a lot more than they are being paid for serving on the jury. There is very little you can do about this. What may seem to them an exorbitant amount is actually not all that unusual. The jurors often hear other experts answer the same questions with even higher amounts. One last point should be made. I have been told that it is not uncommon for lawyers and jurors alike to believe that the more an expert charges, the better he or she must be. I will not vouch for the accuracy of this observation.

GET IT IN WRITING

Whatever you decide to charge, it is prudent to get this figure in writing before you begin to work, especially if this attorney is not one you've worked with before and for whom you are a bit uncertain. You can construct a brief contract agreement, for example, outlining your hourly fee, testimony fee, and the requirement to be reimbursed for travel expenses. It's also wise to include a statement to the effect that your contract is between you and the attorneys, not their clients. This is to protect you and enable you to demand payment even if the client reneges and doesn't pay the lawyers. Sometimes U.S. attorneys provide such a contract after you've negotiated with them, asking you to sign and return it. But you can also construct your own agreement.

LETTERS OF AGREEMENT

Often, particularly in civil cases, attorneys will ask you to send them a letter containing your charges and whatever else they require. In other cases, attorneys will explain that they themselves will prepare an agreement letter containing the fee structure you've outlined and any other requirements that their firm has. It is important that your letter include wording to the effect that your relationship is with the attorney, not with the attorney's client. This is to ensure that any disputes about payment along the line are the attorney's responsibility to resolve. In the United Kingdom this letter is often called *prior authority*.

A Sample Letter of Agreement

Dear (Lawyer):
Thank you for your call of (date). I will be pleased to work with you on this case. You asked me to outline my requirements in this case, which are as follows:

Retainer fee: (amount)

Hourly rate: (amount) per hour, reported by units of hours, half hours and quarter hours

Testimony fee: Daily rate of (amount) for any part of a day spent at court

Expenses: Total travel expenses will be paid in advance of testimony and/or deposition dates

Invoicing: I will bill monthly and expect payment within thirty days of receipt of invoice

Relationship: My business relationship is with you, the attorney, and not with your client

Checks: Please make all checks payable to (your name)

Sincerely yours,

(your name)

One last point about invoicing. I have found that many law firms pay their outstanding accounts at the end of the month. Therefore, if you bill at the end of a month, your invoice gets shuffled to the following month. To ensure payment by the end of a given month, it may be prudent to set your monthly billing date at mid-month.

CONFIDENTIALITY AGREEMENTS

In some instances, again usually only in civil cases but sometimes also in high-profile criminal cases in the United States, attorneys may require the expert to sign a confidentiality agreement written by their office (this is less common in the United Kingdom). These vary somewhat, but they basically indicate that you will not divulge any information related to this case to anyone else. The main purpose of this confidentiality agreement is to assure them that you will not let the opposition get hold of the material they send you, including your notes and analysis, whether preliminary or final. Another reason is to preserve confidentiality about the case from the media or others who may wish to benefit financially from writing about it.

When signing such agreements, one thing to be careful about is whether the agreement you sign only precludes you from using the data and analysis for the length of the case (until its final disposition) or if it precludes any such use in perpetuity (extending after the case is settled). Whenever I have signed a confidentiality agreement and I then decide to write about the case at some time after it's over, I make it a point to write to the attorney for clarification. In most cases, I've been told that I'm free to use the material for academic purposes. In U.S. criminal cases, once the case is resolved, the evidence and all other materials sent to you enter into the public domain, making it perfectly legitimate to use them for papers and books. If there is any doubt about the possibility of you casting participants in a bad light, you can usually anonymize the case, which tends to solve the confidentiality problem. I have done this in certain cases when I was uncertain about the feelings of the defendants or attorneys.

Sample Confidentiality Agreement

Privileged and Confidential
Attorney–Client Communication
Attorney Work Product

Dear (linguistics expert),
This letter confirms our conversations regarding the law firm of (name) retaining you at the rate of (amount) per hour for your knowledge and expertise in forensic linguistics. We agree for you to conduct a linguistic analysis of a portion of the audio and video surveillance evidence compiled by the government in order to aid our trial preparation for (defendant) in connection with this upcoming criminal trial in the United States District Court, (location).

We represent (defendant) in a federal criminal matter. (defendant) has authorized (law firm) to retain you to work under our direction and report directly to us. We agree that you will perform tasks pertaining to this case at the direction of (law firm).

Under this agreement, all communications between us, as well as communications between you and any attorney, agent, or employee acting on our behalf, shall be for the sole purpose of assisting counsel and giving legal advice to (defendant). We agree that you will not disclose to anyone, without our prior knowledge and written permission, the nature or content of any oral or written communication, nor any information gained from the inspection of any record(s), document(s), audio tape(s) submitted to you, including information obtained from corporate records or documents, and you will not permit inspection of any papers, documents, or audio/video tapes without our prior written permission. We further agree that all audio/video tapes, work papers, records, or any other documents you prepare or obtain in the course of this engagement, regardless of their nature and the source from which they emanate, shall be held by you solely for our convenience and subject to our unqualified right to instruct you with respect to possession and control. Work papers prepared by you, or under your direction during the course of this engagement, shall be the exclusive property of this law firm in which you retain no rights.

As part of your agreement to assist us in this matter, we agree that you will immediately notify (law firm) of the happening of any one of the following events: (a) the exhibition or surrender of any audio/video tapes, documents or records prepared by or submitted to you or someone under your direction, in a manner not expressly authorized by this law firm; (b) a request by anyone to examine, inspect, or copy such audio/video tapes, documents or records; (c) any attempt to serve, or the actual service of any court order, subpoena, or summons requiring the production of any such documents or records. We understand and agree that you will immediately return all documents, records, work papers, and audio/video tapes to us at our request.

Enclosed are (tapes), (transcripts) of certain conversations prepared by the government, the Superseding Indictment, affidavits of government agents supporting the search and seizure warrants, a brochure prepared by (defendant's business), and the complaint for forfeiture *in rem*. Pursuant to your request, I have also enclosed a check for (amount) to serve as a retainer. We understand and agree that you will obtain authorization from us prior to incurring a total expense balance (including without limitation charges for materials and hourly fees) in excess of the (amount) retainer.

Please sign the original letter and return it to us for our files.

If you have any questions regarding any of the items discussed in this letter, please do not hesitate to call me. We look forward to discussing your analysis.

Sincerely,
(name of law firm)
(signed by (lawyer)

AGREED TO:
(your name)
(date)

Most of the confidentiality agreements that I've signed are not this complex (and are often more clearly worded). I include it here because it contains most of the things that such agreements deal with.

WHEN YOU ACCEPT A CASE

So now you've reached an agreement about payment and are officially hired. You're off and running! From the start, however, you should be willing to maintain your neutrality and be totally honest about what you find.

Be Objectively Neutral, Not an Advocate

Agreeing to take a case means that you are willing to be an objective outsider to the matter. The first thing to keep in mind is that the job of advocacy is the lawyer's, not the expert's. Your analysis should be the same no matter which side of the case you work for. It's not easy to maintain objectivity once you start working with an attorney advocate, so one needs to learn to be able to point out the downsides of the evidence as well as the good things you can contribute to the case. Doing so actually may be as helpful to the attorney you work with as showing him or her the advantages that your analysis may provide. In any case, there is a fine line between being a helpful collaborator and becoming an advocate (see chapter 8. I also discuss this in my book *Linguistic Battles in Trademark Disputes*, 2002).

Be Willing to Say That a Case Is Hopeless

If you and particular attorneys have worked together in the past and have developed a trusting relationship, telling them that their clients are doomed from day one is a bit easier. I know several attorneys, for example, who feel free to send me undercover tapes of their clients caught in narcotics sting cases. On many occasions, after reviewing the tapes, I tell them that the best thing they can do is to take the best plea bargain they can get. The attorneys are usually grateful for this bad news, because it tells them that their initial instincts are correct and it guides them in dealing with their clients. They didn't expect

magic. On more than one occasion, attorneys have had me meet
with their clients, explaining to them that the language evidence cannot possibly work to their advantage and convincing them to try to try to get a plea bargain agreement.

INVOICING

Most cases go on for several months or more. After you've
used up your retainer, you need to bill for the following work.
In most cases I invoice clients monthly. I also require a siz-
able retainer at the beginning as way of guarding against the
possibility that the lawyer will renege somewhere along the
line. On your own letterhead, you should make your invoice
as simple and clear as possible. It should be sent to your lawyer, not to the client he represents. It should include the hours
spent using up the amount sent you as a retainer.

> ### Sample Invoice
>
> Dear (lawyer's name)
> The following invoice is for work done at your request in
> the case of (name of case, such as *US v. John Doe*), during
> the period from January 1, 2005 to January 31, 2005.
>
> | Jan. 5 | 3 hours |
> | Jan. 6 | 4.5 hours |
> | Jan. 18 | 6 hours |
> | Jan. 20 | 2.5 hours |
> | Jan. 29 | 1.5 hours |

total hours:	17.5 @ (hourly rate)
Total due for this period	$(amount)
Less retainer	–$(amount)
TOTAL DUE AT THIS TIME	$(amount)

Please make check payable to (your name).

Sincerely yours,

(your name and title)

In some cases, the attorney will want you to briefly describe the work done on each of the days. Phrases such as "listened to tapes," "analyzed tapes," "corrected transcript," or "wrote report" will usually suffice.

BEING STIFFED

Stiffed is a term commonly used to describe what happens when you are not paid for work you have contracted to do. I have never been stiffed for the work I did in a civil case, where the clients are often wealthy corporations. Stiffing is more likely to happen in criminal cases, often involving clients who have little money in the first place or who lose it all in their effort to defend themselves. Fortunately this doesn't happen very often, as long as you take steps to guard against it. I estimate that I've been stiffed in only about 1 percent of the cases I've worked on. Usually it's the last payment that becomes the problem. If it's a criminal case and the client gets convicted, the motivation for final payment decreases greatly once he or she goes to jail. He or she may not have paid the attorney either. So timing is important. Be sure to get final payments well in advance of trial. If you are expected to testify at trial, it is prudent to get paid for your travel expenses and fees for giving testimony well in advance.

Most lawyers pay their bills, but some, unfortunately, do not. There isn't much you can do when you are not paid for the work you complete. It helps some (but not a lot) to have made clear that the responsibility for your payment is that of the attorney you work with, not the client. A few conscientious lawyers have paid me out of their own pockets even when their client has stiffed them for some or all of their payment. Other attorneys are simply indifferent or inefficient, which is why I make it a point to get to know the people who work in their offices, especially those in charge of paying the bills. In one criminal case where I testified in Alaska, the attorney was appointed by the state. After his client was convicted, he simply ignored my final invoices. I then began calling his legal assistant, whom I had met at the trial. She became my advocate in the matter and got the lawyer to finally fill out the papers for my payment from the state. Whether the case is civil or criminal, I have found it useful to know the lawyer's staff. Sometimes they can get their bosses to send materials they promised but had overlooked during their immediate crises.

FUTURE WORK: DECIDING WHICH CASES YOU PREFER

After thirty years of forensic consulting, I've worked on virtually all types of civil and criminal cases. Over the years I have

developed personal preferences for the kinds of cases I'll accept. In some types of cases, such as authorship identification
or speaker identification, I find that my work can be used as
an investigative tool to help law enforcement try to narrow
down their suspect lists or for investigators to use as they interview suspects. However, I simply won't take the witness
stand with such analysis until such time as our field can better answer some important questions, including:

- which features are the most important,
- how many such features count toward actual
  identification,
- how to deal with language variability, and
- how to account for the fact that comparison samples are
  not often in the same genre as the offending writing or
  speech.

That is *my* problem, however, and it does not seem to prevent other linguists from addressing such issues on the witness stand.

Suspecting that my American forensic linguistics colleagues had their own preferences and dislikes, I surveyed
25 of them that I know are active in such work. Surgery had
put me out of commission for about six months, and I wanted
to know how best to refer cases to them. I broke the case categories down as follows, which also notes the number of linguists who agreed to accept cases in each category.

criminal activities	15
contract disputes/fraud	14

jury instructions	10
trademark	10
defamation	8
sexual abuse	7
authorship identification	6
perjury	6
copyright/plagiarism	6
sexual misconduct	5
language testing/assessment	5
legal language	5
non-English cases	4
plain language/ERISA	2
voice identification	2

This survey is skewed in many ways and can in no way be understood to be scientific. For example, I didn't survey phoneticians per se, who probably do most of the voice identification work. Each respondent had the opportunity to choose more than one category. Although it represented only linguists that I know, it gave me a clue at least to the kinds of cases that seem to be preferred. Clearly, written language wins over spoken, for example, and civil cases seem to be preferred over criminal cases.

Personally, I have come to prefer criminal cases over civil ones. Perhaps that's because I like the fact that individual freedom is involved rather than matters of financial gain or loss. But that's my opinion and preference. You will need to decide yours because your potential effectiveness may de-

pend on your doing cases you are more comfortable with and
like best.

DECIDING WHETHER TO INCORPORATE

For many U.S. linguists, an occasional consultantship on a law
case is simply additional income to be reported on their personal income tax forms. When they begin to do more cases,
however, the idea of incorporating begins to make sense,
because there are potential tax advantages and benefits issues to think about. The legal structures available are a sole
proprietorship, a partnership, a limited liability company, or
a corporation. If you're thinking about incorporating, you
should get advice from accountants and lawyers to pick the
form that best serves your needs.

A sole proprietorship is the simplest and least expensive
of these, but your profits must be included in your personal
tax form (the same is true for general partnerships). Thus you
are taxed at the same rate as your regular university job. Most
forensic linguists work alone, so the idea of having a general
partnership or limited partnership may not make a lot of
sense. Limited partnerships tend to be most useful for busi-
nesses that invest in other things, such as real estate, again
not particularly relevant to forensic linguistic consulting.

A regular corporation is more expensive to create than sole
or general partnerships, and it requires more burdensome
paperwork. But such corporations operate as a separate tax

entity, and in the United States the rate of tax for corporations is considerably less that for personal rates (usually
about 20 percent as opposed to a much higher rate for personal income). They also permit some fringe benefit possibilities, which can include, for example, purchasing the
books you need, paying for memberships in professional organizations, professional travel, office equipment and sup-
plies, and other expenses that are clearly related to your
consulting work. If the officers of your corporation agree,
they can also agree to pay for all nonreimbursed medical
expenses and medical insurance contracts for all employees, a significant feature these days. I hasten to point out that
the above relates only to the United States. Readers from
other countries will need to investigate the possibilities of
incorporation there.

Soon after I discovered that my consulting practice with
attorneys was rapidly growing, I decided to form a regular
corporation. Over the years I've averaged about 20 law cases
a year, and the regular corporation structure has suited my
needs well. I had to pay the initial costs of forming the corporation, and I have expenses for my accountant, who keeps
my records straight and prepares my tax reports. One nuisance factor is that my corporation has to establish monthly
salaries (which I set based on past experience) for all employees (my wife and me) and pay federal income taxes and
Social Security monthly. If my corporation has money left
over at the end of the fiscal year, I can pay bonuses to any
or all employees, leaving only the minimal amount in the

company's account. It can get complicated if the corporation hires other employees, except for those who earn less that $600 per year. If they earn more than this while working for you, you must send them an annual W2 tax reporting form and submit the same with your company's annual tax report.

4

Working with Attorneys

COMMUNICATION: FACE TO FACE,
E-MAIL, OR TELEPHONE/FAX

Communication is a big issue, especially when there is a long
distance between the linguist and the lawyer. Most attorneys
are busy with their own work on cases, and once they've
asked you to analyze their data, many of them tend to be hard
to reach. Face-to-face meetings are always best, if you can get
their attention long enough to explain your analysis. This is
true mostly in criminal cases but sometimes also in civil cases,
mostly because civil cases have a deeper pocket and usually
have a longer time period for preparation. A lot depends on
the amount of time between when you are hired and when
the trial is scheduled to start. I have found that this amount
of time tends to be much longer in civil cases, providing the
expert more time to analyze and prepare. In criminal cases,
especially if the lawyer doesn't think about the need for a

linguist early on, getting some attention and time to explain your work tends to be difficult.

DISCOVERY CONCERNS

One of the things an expert needs to know about is what the legal profession calls *discovery*. Most cases begin with lawyers making various pleadings. In the U.S. system, there are proceedings before trial for which each side has the right to information about the other side's case. In the United Kingdom, civil cases use the same name for this procedure, but in their criminal cases it is called *disclosure*. The Crown is obliged to make available to the defense every bit of information (except in cases of possible damage to the public interest). The defense does not share the requirement to disclose everything—only that which it plans to use at trial. In U.S. civil cases, the discovery procedure can include taking live testimony of potential witnesses (called depositions). It can also include posing lists of written questions (called interrogatories) and requesting documents in evidence. There is an obvious value in such a process. Once the strength of the evidence is known by both sides, trials are sometimes averted and settlements accepted.

The significance of discovery for the linguistic expert is that whatever documents or other materials are produced must be turned over, or discovered, by the other side. This includes notes of phone conversations, notes taken about the case, drafts of reports, as well as final written reports.

If you are working at a long distance from the attorney, you'll probably have to settle for communicating by e-mail or fax. This is fine as long as there are no discovery restrictions. In U.S. civil cases, it is possible that the draft versions of your work can be discovered by the other side. This is less true for most criminal cases, but the attorney should warn you about specific requirements involved. In some cases, the expert will be told to mark all materials sent to the attorney with the words *work product,* which apparently preserves your work from being discovered (although even this safeguard does not always seem to be effective).

Notes and drafts can pose a discovery problem. Suppose, for example, your initial analysis seems to be taking you in a direction that you later find to be inadequate or even wrong. You correct your direction, but the notes are still there. When you are deposed, such notes, if you still have them, can be discovered by the opposition and used against you in obvious ways. Even your notes of phone conversations with the attorney can be discovered. In the days before electronic writing, even the early drafts of reports or analyses could be discovered. Today it is common practice for experts to use the write-over technique on all draft reports. The earlier versions or wordings are thus no longer accessible for discovery. As a general rule, it's better to have few (if any) notes or old drafts in your possession when you are deposed.

I have found that working with attorneys over the phone is the least satisfactory way to communicate. It's much better to sit with them in their (or your) offices.

TEACHING AND LEARNING

The first task is to get the attorney to understand what your analysis means. You have to do an education job for many of them, because most are usually new to using linguists. But good lawyers are also intelligent and know a great deal about language, because law is essentially about language anyway. They just don't know about linguistics. So teaching the lawyer about your analysis is good practice for eventually teaching a jury when you give expert witness testimony. Practice using nontechnical terms and figuring out ways of showing syntax that don't seem overly complicated. Create drawings or visual illustrations to make your points. I have found that juries are often visual learners, so they tend to understand and appreciate charts and graphs.

PHONE CALLS FROM THE OPPOSING LAWYERS

There comes a time in a most lawsuits when the attorneys are required to provide a list of all the witnesses they intend to call at trial. In several cases that I've worked on, after my name has been revealed as a potential witness, I've received phone calls from the other side, trying to find out what I will say about the case. The first time this happened, I was totally surprised. The attorney I was working with had not informed me about such a possibility. Fortunately, I had the presence of mind (or perhaps suspicion) to tell the other side's lawyer that I would first have to check with my attorney before speaking with her.

On other similar experiences, the attorney I was working with has told me to agree to speak with the other side but to specify that this can happen only if my attorney is also present, either in person or on the telephone. I assume that this approach is to give my attorney the chance to object to questions or to prevent me from telling the other side anything that might compromise the case. The point here is to be aware that such requests may be made and that expert witnesses need to be protected by the attorney with whom they are working.

Such requests from the opposing attorney are less frequently made in U.S. civil cases, where they have the opportunity to learn about the expert's work through reports and depositions. In the United Kingdom, there is a provision under Scottish law known as *precognition*, in which a representative of the other side can visit witnesses and interrogate them on what they will say at trial.

5

Analyzing the Data

THE LAWYERS WILL SEND YOU A PILE OF MATERIAL. Usually it is just what you need, but sometimes you need to ask for things that they didn't send. Often, what you get needs to be organized in ways that you can better deal with it.

ORGANIZING THE MATERIAL

Good organization is the key, especially when the case contains a great deal of material. The following is a list of the types of material you can expect to be sent you in civil and criminal cases.

Criminal Cases
The information sent to the expert witness often includes:

- audio or video tape recordings of undercover conversations
- government-made transcripts of these conversations
- indictment

51

- search warrant
- law enforcement reports of contacts with the defendant
- excerpts of the relevant law pertaining to the case
- written reports of witnesses (sometimes with tape recordings)
- audio or video tapes of police interviews
- government-made transcripts of these interviews
- law enforcement written reports of interviews
- written messages related to the crime, such as letters, suicide notes, hate mail, etc.

In the United States these materials are organized first by the government, using whatever system it might devise. The tapes may be numbered and dated—but not always. The transcripts may be marked with corresponding numbers and dates of the tapes—but not always. Often the dates and numbers are simply inaccurate, causing the defense to have to straighten them out. The reports of the relevant law enforcement agency vary from agency to agency. FBI 302 reports are often brief summaries of what happened in the accompanying tape-recorded meetings. DEA Investigative Background Reports and ATF reports often contain much more detail, sometimes including selected quotes from what they believe to have been said on the tape recordings. Local police reports are a mixed bag of much briefer information, varying in length and quality from jurisdiction to jurisdiction.

Once the indictment is made, this information is then made available by discovery to defense attorneys, who often create their own organization structures to process it. Thus a tape numbered "03555" by the government may be renumbered "10–23–97" by the attorney.

Eventually, the mass of data is sent to the expert linguist, who has to create his or her own system of organizing the material, at the same time trying cross-reference or preserve as much of the attorney's system as possible for efficiency of communication. Getting the historical order of events straight is the first task, because things happen sequentially. Filing separate tape and transcripts in order is crucial.

Once the evidence is in appropriate order, the next step is to listen to the tape recordings and correct the government transcripts where necessary. This is always appropriate, because government transcripts often contain a multitude of errors. Wrong speakers may be attributed, words or phrases may be omitted, words and phrases may be added when they don't appear on the tapes, grammar of the police is sometimes made to look standard, grammar of the defendant may be made nonstandard, along with many other outright mistakes. This is more common in undercover body mike conversations than in intercepted phone calls, but even the latter can contain egregious inaccuracies.

After this preanalysis is completed, the linguistic analysis begins. Here the linguistic tools, such as discourse analysis, semantics, pragmatics, and speech acts, are often most useful in determining whether the words of the defendant indicated guilt, innocence, or indifference.

Civil Cases

The information often sent to the linguistic expert often
includes:

- complaints and countercomplaints
- depositions of participants on both sides
- specific language data at the point of contention
- contracts
- advertisements
- relevant laws and regulations
- relevant case law
- standards made by government regulatory agencies
- manufacturer's operation guides
- hazard labels on packages
- Lexis/Nexis electronic searches
- communications evidence related to the case

Not all civil cases generate all of the above resources, of
course. This list intends only to alert linguists that there can
be a great deal of reading material in addition to the specific
language of the case. But it's not always a bad thing. For example, in a case involving an arcane law permitting U.S. manu-
facturers to obtain a government rebate for products made by
them but shipped overseas, I had the unusual opportunity to
learn more about the growing and packaging of various types
of asparagus than I ever imagined possible.

It can be very useful to understand the basic outlines of
the civil law related to your case. This is particularly true for
trademark cases, where it would be prudent for any linguist

to study McCarthy on trademarks (1997), chapter 11, which attempts to distinguish between the important categories of generic, descriptive, suggestive, and fanciful/arbitrary marks. In most cases, the attorney will suggest other readings related to specific categories of law. It also makes good sense to read some of the forensic linguistics literature on cases relating to the one you work on, just to see how other linguists did it (see references in chapter 13).

Organizing the materials in civil cases is not as complex as it is usually is for criminal cases. Perhaps civil law attorneys are innately more organized. But the materials usually come well marked and comprehensible.

Linguistic analysis in civil cases tends to focus on the use of semantics, discourse analysis, pragmatics, speech acts, and in some trademark cases, phonetics, although other tools also can come into play.

TESTING HYPOTHESES

As you start doing your analysis, you may feel like part of the team you work with. This can be dangerous. Lawyers are, by definition, advocates. They have to work to either defend or attack. But that's not the forensic linguist's role. We are to analyze the data for what it is and not try to twist it to either defend or prosecute. The unstated goal, of course, is to be able to help the attorneys you work with to win their cases—to the extent that your analysis supports this.

For example, if you are called by a defense attorney in a criminal case, it is useful to try to take the prosecution's perspective as well as that of the defense. Criminal cases are made up of two major hypotheses: one of guilt and one of innocence. Obviously, the defense works from the hypothesis of innocence. That's why the defense attorney called for linguistic help in the first place. But it can be dangerous to neglect exploring the government's hypothesis of guilt. Clearly the government believes the defendant is guilty or there wouldn't have been an indictment in the first place. By exploring the hypothesis of guilt, I mean that the linguist should also try to make the prosecution's case, using all the language evidence available. If it can be made, the best thing to do is to report this to the defense attorney you work with. This does not preclude you from doing further work on the case, however, because indictments often are padded with other charges that can be successfully defended. In many of the criminal cases I've worked on, the language evidence could only be used to defend the accused against some but not all of the charges in the indictment.

One of the problems that many prosecutors face is that they approach their cases with only one theory—that of guilt. A good example of a prosecutorial disaster is when the prosecution considered only a single hypothesis of guilt is the case of *U.S. v. John DeLorean* (Shuy, *Language Crimes*, 1993), when millions of dollars of public money was wasted simply because the government was unwilling to entertain any possibility except DeLorean's guilt. Had the prosecutors even tried to put the many tape-recorded conversations into context, they could have anticipated the defense that was coming. As a result, DeLorean was acquitted of all charges, and the prosecutors were stuck with a very large bill, to say nothing of a good deal of egg on their faces.

Alternative hypotheses sometimes also can be tested in civil cases. They help anticipate any linguistic analysis made by the other side, although in civil cases these are usually obvious from the almost obligatory depositions and reports.

BEING READY TO BE ATTACKED

An uncomfortable aspect of working on a criminal or civil case stems from the fact that being an expert witness is an invitation to be attacked by the other side. If you have thin skin, it may not be a good idea to get involved in this work at all. Depositions and trial testimony are not always the fun part of this work. The other side may constantly try to impeach your analysis and even attack you personally—all the more reason to be well qualified and understand the nature of the process. The expert needs to be on guard at all times, ready for the trick questions and sarcasm of the opposing lawyers (see chapter 7 on being deposed and chapter 8 on testifying at trial). If you can take such attacks without blowing up or getting defensive and flustered, you may pass one of the crucial tests of becoming an expert witness. Angry responses do not set well with juries or judges.

TEACHING LINGUISTICS TO YOUR ATTORNEY

One of the most difficult problems of all can be to get the attorney you work with to understand and appreciate your use of linguistics in the case. One objection will be that the jury won't be able to follow your technical analysis. This can be true in some instances, and if your analysis is complex, you would do well to figure out ways to make it simple and clear. This idea tends to be confounded by the familiar work you do inside the field, where the audience consists of fellow linguists who speak the same language and begin with the same presuppositions. In one of my trademark cases, the issue was whether the two trade names sounded alike. The opposition said they did. The attorney I worked with said they didn't. I attempted to use distinctive feature analysis to be able to quantify the different sounds in the two names. Although this preliminary analysis worked very well for my lawyer's case, he felt that it would be too complex for the jury to follow.

The expert has the unenviable task of making the complex become understandable to people who do not know our field. This can be done with homey examples and personal experiences, by avoiding technical terms altogether, or by describing your technical analysis, then restating it in terms that nonlinguists can understand. Even better sometimes would be to first state the analysis in layperson's terms, then restate it technically. In short, you will be teaching a course in baby linguistics.

TIME CONSTRAINTS

Academics are used to working on a research project, paper, or book until they feel that it is finished. There are time constraints of a sort, but not usually ones that are out of their control. In contrast, the time that you have to work on a law case is controlled by the court. Criminal cases usually give you less time to analyze than do civil cases, which are often drawn out for long periods. This is all the more reason to find out exactly when the trial is scheduled before you agree to take a case. Criminal lawyers, more than civil attorneys, sometimes call for experts rather late in the process.

Even once a trial or hearing date is set and you have worked long hours to be ready, there is frequently a last-minute delay. Repeated postponements are not uncommon. Once you realize that this happens with some frequency, there is the temptation to assume it will always happen. Don't make this assumption. Be prepared for the initial date given and consider any additional time as a rare but welcome gift.

If you are also teaching courses or otherwise working at the same time as the law case, the time you have to work on that case may be limited. This matters little to the court. Its schedule becomes your schedule, like it or not. This means that you may not have the satisfaction of doing everything you want to do on a given case. And that means that sometimes you go to trial not as well prepared as you'd like. For this reason, perfectionists may not want to get involved in law cases at all. Or they may want to take only cases that have a reasonably long germination period before they go to trial.

Things can get particularly complicated when you carry more than one case at the same time. I've done this, and it can be difficult but seldom impossible to handle, except for overlapping trial dates. Only once in my life have I been expected to be in two different trials where my testimony was expected on the same day. I worked this out with my attorneys, however, and I testified at one trial in Nevada and then flew to the other trial in Oklahoma that night, testifying on the following day.

For most trials, the court gives a bit of leeway for the expert's schedule. In one case when my schedule called for me to be out of the country on the date of my scheduled appearance at trial, I was permitted to give my testimony on videotape in Washington, D.C. (both direct and cross-examination), which was then played later at the trial in Florida. It was a nuisance for the defense attorney and prosecutor, who had to arrange their own schedules for the taping. But problems like that can be resolved.

REFERENCES

McCarthy, Thomas. 1997. *McCarthy on Trademarks and Unfair Competition*, 4th ed. Vols. 3 and 4. Eagan, MN: West Group.

6

Writing Reports

Once the analysis has been made, the next step in most civil cases usually involves the preparation of a written report, sometimes in the form of an affidavit and sometimes just as a report. The attorney will advise you which form to use. *Affidavits* are legal documents containing a special format that the attorney will provide, including numbered paragraphs and a space to be notarized. *Reports* may seem more familiar in format and contain, on the whole, some similarities to conventional academic writing. For example, they begin with the legal question, much like a academic research question, followed by the type of language evidence, the methods used, and the findings. Not found in reports are the long justification statements that academics often write or the common literature review.

The report or affidavit will form the substance of a deposition (discovery) by the opposing attorney (see chapter 7). Although reports are not required in U.S. criminal cases as frequently as they are in civil cases, the format is generally similar.

DISCOVERY OF MATERIALS

Either form of report writing should be preceded by considerable amounts of communication with the attorney, because
drafts can be discoverable by the other side. Face-to-face
meetings or lengthy phone discussions can be expected. Attorneys have their own preferences about how best to produce a report, but I have found certain conventions to be
common.

STRUCTURE AND ORGANIZATION

Different attorneys have their own ideas about how the report
should appear. I have found that there is some agreement,
however, that the report should be as concise as possible,
because it will be read by judges, who often have little time
or patience.

Your Qualifications

Some (but not all) attorneys want the report to begin with
a paragraph containing a very brief statement about the expert's qualifications (a curriculum vitae is always attached).
This may seem difficult if only because it feels like tooting
your own horn. But that's the way this field operates. We have
to begin by citing all the wonderful things we've accomplished. If you are timid about this, your attorney will see to
it that you comply, because his or her case depends on your

being a wonderful expert with all kinds of qualifications and abilities. Your attorney also wants to forestall the possibility that the opposing lawyer may object to your not being a real expert.

Your Field

The next paragraph is a brief statement defining linguistics, included because many lawyers and judges are not familiar with the field. It isn't necessary to go into detail defining linguistics or the tools you use. Linguistics can be described as a science with accepted scientific procedures. This can be accomplished by noting that linguistics is considered a science by the National Science Foundation, which offers research grants to linguists. If you feel so inclined, you might also mention that the American Association for the Advancement of Science often calls on linguists to speak at its conferences. You could also point out that most major universities have departments of linguistics, and virtually every academic institution has linguists in various departments. You could conclude by pointing out that the goals of linguistics (describing data, making comparisons, discovering structure, making predictions) are the same as the goals of other sciences.

If your description of the field of linguistics includes the various tool areas, you should point out which of these areas you used in the body of the report following. Here you can use a bit more detail about these tools—but not a lot.

Your Basic Conclusions

Your attorney will want you to get to the point right away, and it is usually the case that your conclusions are placed at the beginning of the report, followed by points that highlight your analysis and concluding more or less with a repetition of the opinion you gave in the first paragraph. The term *opinion* is commonly used. To the linguist who has carried out an analysis that seemingly proves something, calling your conclusion an opinion may seem weak and inappropriate. But that's what they call it, and you're stuck with it.

Brevity

Because most expert witness linguists are academics who teach, it is tempting to say more than is necessary in the report. Instead, it is best to simply give the basics, without the many usual illustrations and examples that teachers normally use in the classroom. Keep in mind that it is up to the opposing attorneys to ask for elaboration or examples if they want to delve deeper than what you present in the report. One way to accomplish such brevity is to draft a report with all the bells and whistles you feel necessary and then edit most of them out afterward. You should be careful, however, to include any issue that will be relevant to your testimony. In some cases it may be prudent to add that your analysis is still ongoing.

The less you say in your report, the less the opposing attorneys (in the United States) have to ask you about in your deposition that will surely follow. At that time, if they open the door, you can say what you want. If they don't go in that direction, you can always use your good points on your direct examination at trial, as long as your attorney agrees.

7

Being Deposed

AFTER THE REPORT IS SUBMITTED, AMERICAN LINGUIS-
tic expert witnesses can expect to be deposed by the other
side, whose lawyers will go through each point with a fine-
toothed comb. (The deposition does not exist in the United
Kingdom, where experts can be questioned at trial about their
written reports.) The U.S. deposition is structured so that the
opposing lawyers can try to find out (discover) what you will
say at trial and to provide a record of your work that can be
addressed if you do testify. Their third agenda is to discover
what kind of witness you'll be, whether you can be rattled,
how well you handle tough questions, and how the jury or
judge may regard you as an expert. The deposition is taken
under oath and is usually held in the office of the opposing
attorney. The attorney you work with will be there to object
whenever necessary. Depositions are recorded by a court
reporter, often with an accompanying videotape recording.

Many (but not all) such depositions can be relatively un-
pleasant experiences, because they are not conducted in front

of a judge, and hostile attitudes can be very discomforting. The opposing attorney may try to impeach your testimony or even impeach you personally. The attorney with whom you work will be there, of course, and will make objections to some questions, but unless you are instructed not to answer, you have to respond. When there is an objection and you are instructed to answer anyway, the uncomfortable answer you have to give may actually never be allowed at trial, because unbeknownst to you, the judge will have ruled the question impermissible.

Experienced attorneys commonly spend at least one work day preparing their experts for depositions. By now they have understood your contributions to their cases. Although they have a reasonably good idea about what they think the opposing attorney will ask, it is wise not to depend on this. For example, in a recent deposition, my attorney and I were very surprised by the opposing counsel's line of questions. This case had been going on for several years, not unusual in some civil cases. I had written a report addressing the linguistic issues in the plaintiff's initial complaint, but strangely I was never deposed about it. The plaintiff then produced a new complaint with an entirely different theory of the case. I wrote a new report addressing the quite different linguistic issues posed by the new theory. Meanwhile, the attorney I worked with withdrew the initial reports of all three of his experts, because they addressed the plaintiff's old theory of the case. At my deposition, both this attorney and I expected that I would be questioned on my second report. But this was not what happened. Some 90 percent of the plaintiff's questions to me related to my first report, written some eighteen months earlier and now not the focus of my thinking. Fortunately, my memory of it was reasonably sharp, otherwise the deposition could have ended disastrously.

It is common for the opposing attorney to go through a report systematically, asking what you meant when you wrote certain things, why you didn't say something else, and whether your analysis was valid. The lawyer will have had access to much of your previous testimony in other cases and will ask why you didn't do the same things in this case. In many U.S. jurisdictions the expert is required to submit a list of all cases in which he or she testified or was deposed in the previous four years. It is prudent for experts to refresh their memories of these cases before the current deposition takes place.

The deposition is taken under oath, so it is obvious that the expert can tell only the truth, even when doing so seems to hurt the case of the attorney with whom he or she works. The expert is always subject to penalties of perjury. This is usually not relevant to linguistic analysis, where you follow the conventions of the field and analyze the text. But in matters such as whether you have retained copies of earlier drafts of your reports, notes about what attorney has told you, or whether he or she suggested changes in your report, it can be tempting to stretch the truth a bit. This should be avoided at all costs.

One way to avoid having earlier drafts discovered is to destroy them after they are revised. As noted earlier, modern word processing composition permits overwriting of old drafts, making the originals not producible. The ethics of this is questioned by some, but it has become the standard method of creating products and has become acceptable as an answer when asked where the original drafts may be located. Sometimes, even after the more or less final draft has been completed, either you or the attorney you work with may find wordings to be changed, slight reorganizations, typographical errors, or other changes in the final version. It is best to remember these and admit them when asked. The opposing attorney gains nothing from such truthful admissions, and it gives you the chance to be considered candid and truthful. As to other memory issues, such as what was said in phone conversations, it is often the case that you might not recall everything exactly. Saying, "I can't recall," is permissible, but if you've kept notes of such conversations, you are required to give them to the other attorney.

Unlike most academic discourse, the deposition is strictly a question/answer process. The opposing lawyer has complete control of the structure and flow of the event, and the deponent's role is to respond only to the questions asked. Any wandering into conversational discussion is to be avoided and will probably be stopped by the attorney you work with if it starts to occur. This can be difficult for inexperienced expert witnesses, who are more accustomed to having control of the flow of their classroom and business exchanges.

Fortunately, the attorney whose client you represent is there not only stop to this when it happens but also object to all questions that are unclear, compound, or out of the scope of the deposition. You should be alert for such objections. They are made to help you stop and consider what the questions really were and whether they were actually questions at all.

Needless to say, the attorney with whom you are working is there only to legally protect his or her own client and not you as an expert witness. If you should perjure yourself or otherwise run into legal troubles, it's at your own expense. This happened to me during the DeLorean trial when it was discovered that some of the evidence tapes had been smuggled to the media before the trial. Anyone who had access to the tapes was a suspect, including me. The FBI called me to ask a few questions, and I wisely hired my own lawyer during this event. This turns out to have been a very good idea, because the agents tried to get me to tell them what I was going to testify about at trial. This line of questioning was totally inappropriate, so my lawyer advised me not to answer. I was naturally concerned about this until one of the law clerks at the firm representing DeLorean admitted that he had sold the tapes to the TV station, and I was off the hook. The point here, however, is that the lawyers you work with are not *your* personal lawyers. They represent their clients alone.

In the deposition it's also wise to keep in mind that the questions that appear to be asked of you are really addressed to an unseen audience: the jury who will eventually hear the case. In the same way, the answers you give are not so much to the lawyer who asks them as to that same unseen audience, who will make the ultimate judgments about the case.

Those of us who are teachers are disadvantaged in depositions, because the deposition runs counter to the way we normally operate. Attorney Richard Beizer, of the law firm of Crowell and Moring in Washington, D.C., prepares expert witnesses with what he calls his LUPA technique. It has four steps: Listen, Understand, Pause, and Answer.

LISTENING

The first and most important thing to do is to *listen* to the question. This has proved to be surprisingly difficult for many witnesses. You should not infer what you think the question intends to mean or try to revise it to suit your own response. Never reply, "If what you mean is—." Never be afraid to ask for the question to be repeated. You should never overlap the end of a question, thinking that you anticipate where it is going. Interruptions and overlaps are to be avoided at all costs. For one thing, two people talking at the same time creates great difficulty for the court reporter. Second, it is discourteous to interrupt. Third, you may be totally wrong about where you think the question is headed. Fourth, overlapping the opposing attorney's question makes it difficult for your own lawyer to object to it. So the main job is to listen carefully first.

UNDERSTANDING

Equally important is to *understand* the question. Don't afraid to say, "I don't understand your question." The deposition is not an opportunity for you to display what you know by answering questions that are not asked. Doing this is exactly what the opposing lawyer wants, because such replies can be used to engage you in a new line of questioning. Listen carefully for the who, what, where, when, and why of the questions and answer only those. Be especially alert to questions beginning, "Is it fair to say that—?" Questions with no foundations are also problematic, such as the one a prosecutor asked me in a Texas murder case: "Dr. Shuy, when you did your subjective analysis, what type of recording equipment did you use?" Fortunately I was alert to his unfounded dependent clause, and I explained that my analysis was objective, not "subjective," and that I used a Bang and Olufsen machine.

PAUSING

What you might consider cooperative behavior, such as finishing an unfinished question, is very dangerous in a deposition. Let the attorney finish the question before you answer. Once it is asked, *pause* for what may seem like an overly long time before answering. For one thing, your pause gives the attorney you work with a chance to object if it seems appropriate to do so. Although it may seem odd to pause for a long time in real-life conversation, you should keep in mind that the only real use of a deposition is in its written form, which does not record response time or pause lengths. While pausing, ask yourself if you really know the answer and how you know it. Never guess. Is your answer based on personal knowledge or from discussions with your attorney? In a recent deposition concerning my analysis of documents in a contract fraud case, I was asked how I knew what *BAFO* and *RFP* meant. I answered that I am familiar with "best and final offers" and "requests for proposals" from my own past experience in submitting grant applications. In contrast, when I was asked how I knew what ceiling price quotes meant, I admitted that I learned the meaning by asking the attorney I was working with. When asked how I knew the meaning of decrements, I replied that I looked it up in a dictionary. All of these methods of discovering the meanings of the specialized language of government contractors were perfectly legitimate. As an outsider to this business, I was not expected to know these things, and the methods I used to find out were perfectly acceptable.

ANSWERING

Be alert for questions ending with tags such as, "didn't you" or "wasn't it." Discourse analysts know that tag questions intend to influence the answer in the way it was stated before the tag. Lawyers know that it's very hard to disagree with the premise of a tag question. Among other things, the listener first has to temporarily suspend belief in the cooperative principle of conversation (Grice 1977). Linguistic experts should have no problem with this, right? But it's one thing to know this academically and quite another to have it happen to you in a deposition, where your mind is racing about many other things.

Also be alert for questions containing allness terms (Osgood 1960), such as "So you always—" or "So you never—." It is unlikely that anything is "always," "never," or "none." You can be relatively certain that questions containing allness terms are carefully constructed to box you in for follow-up queries.

It is entirely likely that the opposing lawyer will pose inelegant questions. If they are vague or ambiguous, allow time for the lawyer you work with to object and ask for a rephrasing. If this doesn't happen and you feel that the question is vague or ambiguous, you are perfectly within your rights to say that you don't understand the question and would like to have it rephrased.

You should answer all questions truthfully, remembering that you are under oath (which the opposing attorney will remind you about several times throughout the process, more to discombobulate you than anything else). And, of course, you should never give answers that go beyond the scope of the specific question.

One effective way to be sure that you're answering only the question asked is to repeat the question aloud before you answer it. Alternatively, you can incorporate the question into the beginning of your response. This is a mental guide to you to answer only the question asked—nothing more, nothing less. If you know that there is more to the question than is asked, leave it to the opposing attorney to think of this. If he or she doesn't, and it's really important, the attorney you work with can bring it up on cross-examination when the adversary's turn is over.

One of the worst ways to answer a question is by guessing at the answer. You should never say, "I'm not sure but—" or "My best guess is—." On the other hand, hedging your answer with appropriate uncertainly can sometimes protect you from the responsibility of being completely accurate. For example, saying "to the best of my recollection" puts the onus on your memory, not your veracity. If the question relates to a written document, even one you wrote yourself, you have every right to ask to see it to refresh your memory. If the lawyer refuses to do so, you can always say, "to the best of my recollection at this time," or something similar. A deposition is not meant to be a memory test, although it often seems to be used that way.

It is not unusual that some time during the deposition you feel that you are caught in some type of self-contradiction or even a mistake. As Beizer puts it, you're out on a limb and you can hear it cracking. In such cases it's best to find your way back to the tree trunk by pausing and listening to the way you feel. Reformulate the question in your own

mind or even aloud if you want. Remember that the tree
trunk of safety is the truth, even if you have to admit to self-
contradiction or error. It may seem like a horrible gaffe on
your part, but the consequences of trying to hide it are usually much worse than admitting the truth. You may get a sinking feeling that you've let your attorney down, but you should
know that lawyers are quite used to such events. Anyway,
it's not at all likely that the case will be either won or lost
by your deposition testimony. It's possible that when it's
your attorney's turn at the end of the deposition, he or she
will try to "rehabilitate" your answer. The very worst that
can happen, even if you feel totally demolished, is that you
will not be used as an expert at the trial. But even the worst
gaffes usually don't lead to such actions.

One important benefit of being deposed is the experience
you can gain from it. A few weeks after it's over you will
probably get a printed copy of the entire deposition to review for any transcription errors. You can't change the
substance of what was said, but you can correct the court
reporter's mistakes in words or spellings. As for the weak-
nesses that you note in your answers, the most useful thing
to do is to think about how you could have responded dif-
ferently. It is prudent for you to make a copy of this printed
version of your deposition and review it when you are deposed in some other later case. In future depositions there
is a good chance that you may be asked about what you said
in this one.

WHAT TO DO IF THINGS GET NASTY

There is likely to come a time when the opposing attorney may try your patience or enflame your emotions. You should always keep in mind that jurors appreciate and value witnesses who can keep their composure. You should practice treating any rudeness or sarcasm calmly: "No sir (or ma'am), that's not what I said." You might even take the lawyer's perspective: "I may not have been as clear as I could be. Let me repeat what I said." This can be a good chance to recycle one of your important points without appearing to be repetitive.

When the opposing lawyer's tactics become obvious, the attorney you work with may object that you are being badgered. At trial the judge could issue a warning about such offensive behavior. But there is no judge present in the deposition. When badgering or sarcasm occurs, witnesses should always pause long enough to let their own attorney do the work of objecting to it. It's their job, not yours, to do the infighting.

Not all opposing lawyers ask questions that are sarcastic or nasty. Sometimes they simply pose trick questions, often ones that try to hide suppositions inside of dependent clauses. Not being alert to these can lead to trouble. They are permitted to ask leading questions as well, including tag questions. With most witnesses, this habitually works well for them. Linguists, who know full well how tag questions work, should not be so easily tricked by them.

Take the cues of attorney you work with about where to sit during the deposition. If there is a video camera present, you will obviously be seated opposite it. Your attorney may suggest that he or she sit opposite the opposing attorney, for strategic reasons. Don't just take the first seat you see. Let the attorney you work with direct the seating arrangement.

REFERENCES

Grice, H. P. 1977. "Logic and conversation." In P. Cole and J. Morgan (eds.), *Syntax and Semantics*. San Diego: Academic Press, 3:41–85.

Osgood, Charles E. 1960. "Some Effects of Motivation on Style in Encoding." In Thomas A. Sebeok (ed.), *Style in Language*. Cambridge MA: MIT Press.

8

Giving Testimony in the Direct Examination

Most civil and criminal cases never go to trial. It is estimated, in fact, that some 90 percent of criminal and criminal cases end before any testimony has to be given. Criminal cases can end with a plea of guilty, a negotiated plea agreement, or a dismissal of charges. Civil cases are often settled with agreements by both parties, often involving the exchange of sums of money. My own experience bears this out. I have testified in only 10 percent of all the cases I've worked on over the past 30 years.

THE SUBPOENA

In some cases and with some types of witnesses, the court issues a *subpoena*, which is a legal-looking request by one of the parties for you to appear in court on a certain day. In my years as an expert witness, I've received only three or four of these. It appears to be more common for the opposing parties to work out a schedule with their witnesses and simply negotiate their agreement to appear on the given date. Civil cases seem to take this approach habitually. Criminal cases may serve subpoenas, depending on the jurisdiction, the nature of the case, and perhaps other things that only the lawyers know. In one criminal case, long after the attorney and I had agreed on when I would testify, I received a subpoena verifying this in the mail. In all of the cases when I've been called to testify before the U.S. Senate or House of Representatives, I have received very nice, certificate-like documents, suitable for framing, signed by the senators and congressmen in charge of the matters, which were actually subpoenas. My notice to appear as a witness in an International Tribunal of Rwanda was a short, simple letter from that office. It would seem that it is rare for a linguist expert witness to be subpoenaed in the United States at least. Following is a characteristically legalistic subpoena that I once received.

Sample Subpoena

(name of court)
To: (your name and address)
Greetings. Pursuant to lawful authority, YOU ARE HEREBY COMMANDED to appear before (court name) on the matter of (case name) on (date and time) at the (place of trial) and then and there to testify about your knowledge in the cause before (name of court). Hereof fail not, as you will answer your default under the pains and penalties in such cases made and provided.
To (counsel you work for) to serve and return.
Given under my hand, this (date)
(signature of presiding officer or judge)

ORIENTATION TO THE COURTROOM

It is a very good idea to have a visual familiarity with the layout of the courtroom before you're called to testify. Linguists who speak at conferences usually like to preview the room where they will speak, noting such things as the distance from the audience, the availability of the electronic equipment to the podium, and other things to make them more comfortable when they give their talks. There is every bit as much reason to become acquainted, even comfortable, with the courtroom where your testimony will be given.

Not all courtrooms are alike. It is comforting to get the layout of the room before you testify, if it is possible to do this. One way is to visit the courtroom when it is empty. Attorneys may be able to arrange such a visit for you. But if this doesn't happen, you can usually get at least a glimpse into most courtrooms through a window at the door and observe the general arrangement. Note where the witness stand is located, where the jury sits, where the judge's bench stands (almost always elevated at the far end of the room), where the attorney's tables are located, and whether there is a podium behind which the attorneys ask their questions. If you are testifying at a preliminary hearing or if the parties have waived trial by jury, then you will be talking primarily to the judge. Consider how much turning you may have to do to face the judge when responding to questions. A simple foreknowledge of the physical context can give you confidence and assurance.

It is also useful (though not always possible) to test the sound system of the courtroom in advance of your testimony.

Most of the time, however, this has to be done by you alone once your testimony starts. Not all sound systems are alike, and you may need to adjust the distance between your mouth and the microphone placed before you. It isn't likely that anyone will adjust the sound system to pick up soft voices, and it's a very bad situation when the jury can't hear you well. This is also a constant reminder to not lean back in your witness chair when you speak. A moderately loud voice indicates confidence, a quality that you want to express.

I have found that giving expert witness testimony in the direct examination is not as strenuous as either the deposition or the cross-examination can be. For one thing, you can plan your direct testimony well ahead of time with the attorney who will direct it. This attorney can also provide you with estimates of the focus of your cross-examination. The cross-examination will likely be more civilized than the deposition, because it is before a judge and jury and the other side's attorneys will usually not want to appear crude or disrespectful. Like you, they are also trying to make a good impression on the jury and judge.

OFFER OF PROOF

Before experts are admitted in many American courts, the attorney is required to present an offer of proof, sometimes called a *proffer*. This is sometimes done in writing before the witness appears. On other occasions the offer of proof is made in a hearing with your attorney before the judge, as the first order of business before the witness even takes the stand. It is very important that the expert linguist be involved in the preparation for this process because the attorney must know exactly what you will and will not say.

If the attorney plans to produce a written offer of proof, the expert should ask to review it carefully, making sure that it doesn't promise things that can't or won't be a part of the eventual testimony. Sometimes the attorney doesn't understand how far the testimony can go or even exactly what it will be. If the offer of proof is given at a preliminary hearing, it is important that the expert be part of it. More than once an offer of proof was made while I was still waiting outside the courtroom. After at least one such hearing I later learned that my testimony would not be accepted by the judge. The reasons for this rejection, later revealed to me, were based on the lawyer's inadequate and even erroneous representation of what my testimony actually would be.

WAITING, THEN BEING CALLED TO THE STAND

Standard practice in criminal cases, and sometimes in civil cases, requires the witness to wait outside the courtroom for the proper time to be admitted. This can be frustrating, but waiting is part of the game. I've waited outside for as long as two days, and the wait is always at least a few hours. When the bailiff finally calls you to the stand, it is best to walk confidently and professionally toward the bench, stopping just before it to be sworn in by the bailiff or clerk, after which you pause briefly, waiting for the judge to tell you to take the witness's chair. When you are told this, it is a good idea to say, "Thank you, your honor." Remember that the jury and judge are sizing you up from the time you enter the courtroom.

While you wait outside the courtroom, various people will likely walk by or be standing around. It is good to remember that you are not to speak with jurors at any time. The problem is that you can't know who the jurors are unless they wear badges identifying themselves. Nor are you to talk with other witnesses, even though you might not know who they are. So the best thing to do is to talk with nobody while waiting. You can silently review your forthcoming testimony in your mind, but it is not wise to refer to any materials while waiting to be called. You never know who will see you, including people working for the other side. If they see you reading your notes, you may expect to be asked on the stand what it is that you were reading. To avoid this, it's best not to have any notes with you in the waiting area. Newspaper reading is relatively safe, but you should avoid reading detective novels or anything that might be even loosely associated with the trial at hand.

In preliminary hearings, when you might be able to wait inside the courtroom, leave everything you won't need (your coat, briefcase, etc.) on the bench next to you. Be ready to stand up immediately when the judge enters and leaves the courtroom. You need to be ready to approach the witness stand the minute you are called without fumbling with your belongings.

TEACHING, AT LAST

The major task of the expert witness is to teach the jury (or in trials conducted only before a judge, called *bench trials*, the judge) how to understand the way your analysis works in the case. This will probably require you to step back from your academic stance and take on the job of explaining your contribution in terms and concepts that listeners can comprehend. Remember the experiences you've had in teaching introductory courses in linguistics.

Direct examiners tend to ask open-ended questions that give you a chance to expand appropriately but not in an overly long fashion. Their questions are not allowed to be suggestive or leading—quite the opposite of the cross-examiner's line of questions to you. The freedom given the expert by open-ended questions permits teaching to take place naturally. The experts' problem with such freedom is that they are tempted to teach too much, often going into detail that is not necessary to make their points effectively. The direct exam is the place to make points concisely, always keeping in mind the main point to be taught. Then stop. If the attorneys giving the direct exam feel that more should be said, they will ask for it.

DEMEANOR

Polite demeanor should be stressed at all times. If you address the judge, call him or her "your honor." Dress should be equivalent to that of the attorneys. For a male witness, this means a dark-colored suit (not a sports coat), a white shirt, and a conservative tie. For a female witness, this means a dark-toned, conservative work suit with low heel shoes (not spikes or flats) and very little (if any) jewelry. All questions should be treated politely, in the manner of a professional. You should sit straight and address your answers to the jury as much as possible, especially when giving answers that are long. Look at them but never try to curry their favor. Your testimony gives the best impression. By the time you take the stand, they have already seen other witnesses and are making their own comparisons.

From the witness chair it is sometimes virtually impossible to see the judge, but if he or she should intervene at some time and direct a question or comment to you, you should turn around and face him or her when you reply. If you are testifying with no jury present, then attempt to turn at least occasionally to face the judge when responding to questions from the bench. The judge is the person you need to convince. This also helps break your eye contact with the opposing lawyer. Thanking the judge is obligatory when appropriate.

Address forms of the participants are also important. A defense attorney may refer to the defendant using a formal address form, such as "Mr." or "Ms." This puts a face on the defendant. The opposing side may try to depersonalize by calling referring to "the defendant." Notice and use the address forms used by the attorney you work with in your report, during the deposition and during the trial.

QUALIFICATION

According to law, an expert is anyone who has the education, training, experience, and information that can assist the jury or judge better understand the law case. In many areas, the amount of education necessary to be considered an expert varies considerably. For example, an automobile mechanic can be considered an expert in some product liability cases. But when academic areas are of concern, a certain authority is commanded by a maximum amount of education. As mentioned earlier, for linguistics this usually means a doctorate degree, with relevant publications and presentations as evidence of such authority.

The first part of your direct examination testimony will be to get you qualified. Your attorney will ask you to tell the court all the wonderful things that qualify you to be an expert. This can be a bit embarrassing, because it requires you to appear to be bragging, something that may be foreign to your usual experience as an academic. It can be very helpful for the attorneys you work with for you to prepare a question/answer sequence that they can use. After your qualification period is over, the opposing lawyer may try to challenge some of your qualifications. At this point you can see the importance of my early points about achieving expert status to be considered one. Following is a sample qualification.

Q: Dr. (name), what academic degrees do you hold?

A: A PhD in linguistics from (name) University, a masters degree in linguistics from (name) University, and a bachelors degree in (name) from (name) College.

Note what has happened so far. Your attorney calls you "doctor." Many attorneys have pointed out to me that "doctor" is preferred over "professor," because the latter connotes to many people the stereotype of absent-mindedness or the eccentric professor. No matter how egalitarian you may be, insisting that you be called "Mr." or "Ms." in U.S. courts suggests that you don't have advanced qualifications. Note also that the witness begins with the highest degree, then mentions the previous lower ones. If you've had postgraduate training, it may be wise to include it as well. The qualifying then continues.

Q: Dr. (name), what academic positions have you held?

A: Since 1990 I have held the rank of professor of linguistics at (name) University. Before accepting this position, I was associate professor of linguistics at (name) University between 1985 and 1990.

Q: Have you published academic papers and books?

A: Yes, I've authored (number) of papers in various academic journals and (number) of books, mostly in the areas of (name) and (name). [Note: If you don't know the number of these, count them up ahead of time.]

Q: During your academic career have you received grants from federal agencies or private foundations?

A: Yes, I've been awarded (number) of such grants for research [name them if it seems useful].

Q: Have you served on editorial boards of academic journals?

A: Yes, I currently serve on the editorial boards of (number) academic journals [name them if it seems useful].

Q: Are you a member of any learned societies in linguistics?

A: Yes, I am a member of (names) [also mention any offices held].

Q: What honors have you received during your career?

A: [List any; if you have none, be sure that this question isn't asked.]

Q: Have you ever testified in court as an expert in linguistics?

A: Yes [if you have], (number) of times in civil and criminal cases [if you have not, have the question revised to cases you've consulted on, if any].

Q: What is linguistics?

A: Linguistics is the scientific study of language. Like all sciences, linguistics discovers structure and principles. In the case of linguistics, these structures and principles relate to language. Also, like other sciences, linguists analyze various components or levels of language. In our field, these include the sound system (phonology), the way words are formed (morphology), the way sentences are structured (syntax), the structure of meaning (semantics and pragmatics), the way larger discourse is structured (discourse analysis), how language changes over time, and the relationship between language use and social structure (sociolinguistics).

Note here that this is a very minimal description of linguistics. It might seem nice to give a longer one, but for the purpose of this part of your testimony, a short version is adequate.

The point is not to teach a course in linguistics but rather to let the jury know that the field is a legitimate science. This is to forestall the possible accusation that the field is only an unscientific bunch of subjective interpretations. This answer also sets the stage and gives a context for a more detailed accounting of the particular linguistic tools you selected for use in this case. You don't want to say too much too soon.

Q: Is (one of these fields that frames most of your testimony) an integral part of linguistics?

A: Yes it is. [Explain in more detail about this area of linguistics.]

Q: You described linguistics as a science. What evidence is there that it is regarded as a science?

A: Perhaps the best evidence is that the U.S. federal government recognizes linguistics as a science. The National Science Foundation includes linguistics as one of the behavioral and cognitive sciences that it supports with an annual budget for competitive research grants in the sciences. The American Association for the Advancement of Science includes linguistics in its programs, and the National Institutes of Health also funds linguistic research.

Since these organizations are specifically American, corresponding groups should be used in the context of other countries. The attorney you work with may want to go into your qualifications more deeply, perhaps highlighting one or two of your publications if they relate to the case. As you think about the *Daubert* rules (see later discussion on admissibility), you may also want to stress that the books and articles you've written are peer-reviewed and evaluated.

If this goes well, the lawyer on the other side may try to stop the qualification procedure by saying, "Your honor, we accept this witness as an expert in his or her field." If this happens early in the qualification, the attorney you work with may be disappointed, because he or she wants to get all of these good things known to the jury. Obviously, the opposing lawyer does not.

VOIR DIRE

Voir dire is a French phrase meaning " to speak the truth." It works both as a noun phrase and as a verb. Most people associate *voir dire* with the process of weeding out jurors, but it can also occur at the end of the expert's qualification before testimony. It gives the opposing attorney a chance to disqualify the witness (sometimes this is called impeaching the witness—not a very appealing term).

In criminal cases it is common for the opposing attorney to *voir dire* the witness after the qualification phase ends. This is a time for that attorney to try to downplay your qualification to testify in the case. Attention may be paid to your lack of experience, the relevance of your field, or some aspect of your personal history. Sometimes this can approach absurdity, as when one lawyer who asked me for permission to let him

access my high school and college records. On another occasion a lawyer asked me how old I was (I was sixty-two at the
time) and then pointed out that as a male of this age, my hearing was obviously impaired. Some lawyers will try anything.

Don't be confused by the various ways *voir dire* is pronounced in different parts of the country or world. The French
pronunciation often gets quite mutilated, often rather
humorously.

ADMISSIBILITY BY THE AMERICAN COURTS

One important issue facing linguists who are expert witnesses
in the United States is the tests of admissibility now in existence. This is a matter for the lawyer you work with to address,
but it is important for you to be aware of what it involves so
that you can be prepared to deal with it. There are no equivalent admissibility tests in the United Kingdom, where admissibility is more loosely defined. There it is the experts'
qualifications, not their methodologies, that are weighed for
admissibility.

Until 1993, nearly all American jurisdictions applied a
simple standard concerning the admissibility of expert witnesses: The expert should be qualified as an expert in that field,
and testimony must be relevant to an issue in dispute in a case.
The scientific theory or technique must be shown to be generally accepted by the relevant scientific community. If these
requirements were met, the expert's testimony was admissible

in court. The general acceptance test (originally adopted in the 1923 decision of *Frye v. Untied States*) began to be criticized in recent years. It was said to overlook the historical reality that as sciences make progress, many of its theories and techniques are ultimately found to be flawed and unsound. This test also disallowed acceptance of reliable methods that were not yet generally accepted by the scientific community merely because they were too new to be well known.

In 1993 a new standard for admissibility of expert witnesses emerged in the form of the U.S. Supreme Court's ruling in *Daubert v. Merrell Dow Pharmaceuticals, Inc. Daubert* replaced the general acceptance test with a reliability assessment, an independent judicial evaluation of the reliability of the proposed testimony. Reliability was defined by the court as an assessment of whether the reasoning or methodology underlying the testimony is scientifically valid and whether that reasoning or methodology can properly be applied to the facts in issue. The court suggested four factors to assist in the inquiry:

Factor 1. Whether the theory or technique has been tested and found to be sound.

Factor 2. Whether it has been subjected to peer review and publication.

Factor 3. Whether, in respect to a particular technique, there is a high known or potential rate of error and whether there are standards controlling the technique's operation.

Factor 4. Whether the theory or technique enjoys gen-
       eral acceptance within the relevant scientific
       community.

The court advised that these criteria are not fixed or invari-
able. They are flexible and are meant to be helpful rather than
definitive. The four factors are paraphrased from the case
cited above, *Daubert*.

Since 1993, this four-part reliability assessment was appli-
cable to all federal court proceedings involving scientific testimony and has been adopted by an increasing number of
state courts. Some states have hybrid standards involving
both *Frye* and *Daubert*. For a few years, there was considerable confusion about *Daubert*, including its scope. Questions
were raised about whether it applied to only scientific testing and analysis or whether it applied to all forms of expert
testimony, including such areas as engineers, automobile
mechanics, and therapists.

In 1999, the U.S. Supreme Court ruled in *Kumho Tire v.
Carmichael* that the *Daubert* reliability assessment applies to
all forms of expert testimony, not just to a narrow category
of scientific tests. This ruling continued the qualification that
the *Daubert* test was meant to be helpful, not definitive. This
assessment has proved to be most helpful at the extremes of
science. At one end there is the reliability of DNA testing now
accepted by all courts. At the other end there is the rejection
of astrology and palmists. The problem remains for many
fields somewhere in between those extremes. The courts still

struggle with many types of social and human science expertise, such as expertise in the reliability of eyewitness testimony, repressed memory, disassociative disorders, and many others. There is reason to believe that some version of the U.S. *Daubert* and *Kumho* standard is (or will be) gradually crossing the ocean to the United Kingdom, although at the time of this writing nothing formal has occurred. Some courts are not certain about how to deal with linguists as expert witnesses. Our field falls neither in the category of immediately acceptable DNA experts at one end of the spectrum nor in the category of the immediately unacceptable so-called junk sciences at the other end. In short, we have to help attorneys make their cases for linguistic testimony. Stressing the scientific nature and credentials of our field helps with Factor 1. Mention of publications and peer reviews helps with Factor 2. The issue of general acceptance of our field, Factor 4, can be helped by the fact that virtually all respectable universities have linguistics departments.

A larger problem comes from Factor 3, potential rate of error and standards controlling the methodology, a factor that favors experimental sciences over others. Many social sciences appear to have problems with this one. You and the attorney you work with will need to learn ways to deal with it. Factor 3 appears to assume that the sciences are uniform in their definition of the scientific method. One apparent assumption underlying this factor is that commonly the hard sciences create a body of knowledge resulting from the performance of replicated controlled experiments in a laboratory. This is an overly narrow definition of science, because it ignores the equally important comparative method used in many fields. In much of social science research it is impractical or even impossible to carry out laboratory experiments. This is especially true when the data being studied are naturalistic rather than artificially constructed for control. Some judges, particularly those who would like to save trial time by excluding experts, may use Factor 3 as the best way to deny the admissibility of linguists.

Linguists may also be called on to analyze data in specific cases for which the linguistic issue has never before been researched. For example, suppose you are asked to determine whether a taped conversation is staged or natural. If linguists haven't researched this issue before, then the obvious thing to do is compare what is known about naturally occurring conversation with the conversation on the allegedly staged tape. This approach follows the comparative method of science, but it cannot be replicated with naturally occurring language in an experiment. In such cases, the linguist might help the attorney by carefully reviewing the *Daubert* and *Kumho* decisions. For example, one sentence in the *Kumho* decision says, "It might not be surprising in a particular case, for example, that a claim made by a scientific witness has never been the subject of peer review, for that particular application at issue may never previously have interested a scientist" (*Kumho Tire Company v. Carmichael*, 526 U.S. 151).

THE QUESTION/ANSWER FORMAT

I have found it useful to prepare my own version of a question/answer format that I'd like the lawyers I work with to use in my direct examination. Sometimes they agree to most of it, because doing so saves a lot of time and effort for everyone. The questions you'll be asked and the best sequence for them should be worked out well in advance of your testimony. If the attorney asks you some new questions for which you have not prepared and are not comfortable, you have to be alert and not get flustered. I have had the experience of an attorney asking me questions that I thought we had agreed not to get into, because they were inappropriate for my need to steer clear of issues that are the sole province of the jury to decide. The simple answer in such cases is to say simply, "I can't answer that because it's up to the jury to deal with it." Your attorney may not be happy, but your integrity is preserved and, oddly enough, your answer may actually help the case rather than hurt it, because it shows that you are following the rules of a good expert witness.

If your attorney simply forgets the agreed-on plan or rearranges its sequence, you should have prepared so well that you can follow the new arrangement. This has happened to me more than once. In one solicitation to murder case, in my direct examination the attorney failed to ask me about what we had both considered the most important part of my testimony. I was deeply puzzled by this, but I went along with him just the same. As it turns out, he had decided to leave it out deliberately, knowing that it would be the first question asked of me by the prosecutor on cross-examination. He was quite right to use this sandbagging strategy. When the prosecutor asked me about it, I was ready to deal with it and, in the long run, this tactic proved to be very successful.

KEEPING IT SIMPLE AND CLEAR

One distinct advantage that linguists have when they testify is that the information is still new to judges and juries alike. They often get bored with the slow pace of legal argument and the dullness, even predictability, of what many witnesses have to say. When a linguist is involved, they are likely to get refreshingly new information. Some of them even like to learn new things, and trials don't often provide this kind of stimulus. Judges in particular bore easily. So the linguist expert witness starts out with a distinct advantage, simply because our field is so novel to them.

The general advice given by most lawyers is that your testimony should be couched in words and sentences that are easily understood by jurors with an eighth-grade education. Obviously some jurors are better educated, but they are not likely to be educated in linguistics, which is a new area for them to think about. The linguist's problem always concerns how to express complex ideas simply enough to be understood by outsiders to our field. When you talk about syntax, it is helpful to start with grammatical terms that jurors might recall from their seventh-grade English class, such as "simple and compound sentences." Having established this, you might then say something about the way linguists deal with such concepts. This can build a bridge between what they already know, or think they know, and the more complex ideas you want to convey.

You should always explain the technical terms of linguistics in simple terms. For example: "The recency principle means that when people are presented with a number of propositions in the same utterance, they tend to respond to the last in the series, or the most recent one." When it comes to explaining the sounds of English, I have found that juries can be fascinated when you use a cut-away facial diagram of the vocal passages and show how some sounds are produced at the front of the mouth, others in the back, and some more central. Even nasalization can be explained visually much better than with words.

In a bribery case many years ago, there was a dispute between the prosecution and the defense about what a speaker in a tape-recorded conversation actually said. The prosecutor claimed that one defendant said to another, "I would take a bribe, wouldn't you?" The tape was made in a noisy restaurant, making the speech difficult to make out, but many listenings to the tape led me to testify that what the man said was, "I wouldn't take a bribe, would you?" I was able to convince the jury that my reading of this was accurate when I played the tape to them and asked them to count the number of syllables before and after the junctures in each sentence. To assist in this I used a chart containing only the following:

	I would	take a bribe		wouldn't you	
5 syllables •	•	• • •	+ 3 syllables	• •	•
	I wouldn't	take a bribe		would	you
6 syllables •	• •	• • •	+ 2 syllables	•	•

Having asked the jury to count the syllables before and after the junctures, I then explained why the prosecutor's transcript was in error. There was no need for me to go into topics of supersegmental phonology, theories of syllabicity, or any other technical matters.

AIDING YOUR MEMORY: CHARTS AND GRAPHS

Most complex cases contain mountains of data that can pose serious memory problems for the witness to manage. Experts in the United States are usually advised to take no notes with them when they take the witness stand. On first blush, one feels a bit vulnerable up there with no ammunition, while the attorneys on both sides sit at their tables with stacks of notebooks and papers to call on when they need them. Much of the linguist's analysis is done on large units of written or spoken speech.

It's obviously difficult to memorize all of this—and it's not really necessary. One solution to the problem of remembering all the data is to include charts as part of your testimony. When the attorney asks you, "In what ways did your analysis show that the document was ambiguous?" you can respond that you have a chart prepared to show this. Although charts and graphs are less commonly used in the United Kingdom, lawyers in the United States will then ask to have the chart admitted, and the judge almost always agrees. The lawyer places the chart on an easel, and your questioning about it begins. All the language that you want to testify about is right there before you, the jury, and the attorneys to see. It is often necessary for you to leave the witness chair and approach the easel, where the attorney will ask you the questions while you stand there. Before you leave the stand, however, it is common for either you or the attorney to request the judge's permission for you to move there.

The easel on which the charts are displayed should face the jury, making it something of a problem for others to see. Opposing lawyers may walk over to a spot where it is visible to them. If the judge joins them in moving down from the bench, you can infer that what you have to say has created considerable interest. When the charts are homemade, you should be sure that they are legible enough to be read at a distance of around 20 feet.

After you've finished with the charts, you return to the witness stand for follow-up questions. The meat of your presentation now has been visibly represented on the charts, giving the jury the advantage of both seeing your analysis on paper as well as hearing it from you. It has been said that people remember what they see better than what they hear and that they are convinced more by what they hear than what they see. Using charts, you can appeal to both avenues of understanding at the same time.

Most commonly in the United States, charts are used for demonstrative purposes. This means that the jurors are not allowed to take them into the jury room when they deliberate, all the more reason to have a visible representation of your analysis before them as you testify. Your charts provide the memory of all the details, quotations, definitions, and other things that are otherwise difficult to remember. It is wise to make them as simple and legible and readable as possible. You want the jury to remember what they see and be convinced by what you say. This two-prong approach to convincing a jury usually works well.

In recent years charts have been replaced by PowerPoint or other electronic methods. However efficient these may be, they lack something that the old-fashioned handmade chart can offer. For one thing, a handmade chart can be more familiar and comfortable to jurors. Many of them are more accustomed to things like that. Second, if you make the charts yourself, the product can add a bit of your personal association with the case that the professionally made PowerPoint often lacks. In virtually all the trials when I used charts I had made myself, one of the first questions asked by the opposing lawyer was, "Who made these charts for you?" When I responded that I made them myself, the eyes of the jury told me that they were impressed. I am a fairly good artist, and I can make readable lettering. Maybe others can't do this as well, but I believe that homemade versions sell better than electronic ones. For those not comfortable with lettering and drawing, parts of a chart can be made by PowerPoint and enlarged and mounted.

Overheads can come close to the advantages of hand-lettered charts. One disadvantage is that they disappear from view once they are taken off of the screen, while paper charts can remain there longer for the jury to see. An advantage is that I have found that, like hand-made charts, my manipulating the overhead projector places me into the testimony better than the electronic technique, which seems more disconnected with me and what I have to say. In contrast, often PowerPoint can require darkening the room, causing you to lose direct connection with the jury. Finally, the newer technology, for all its supposed advances, currently is seldom used without foul-ups. It is not good for the expert to be seen fumbling around.

When you take the witness stand, you can have your report with you, along with your curriculum vitae and any other exhibits to be used. Be sure that you've tagged and highlighted key points. Keep in mind that any materials you have that the opposing attorney doesn't have, including your notes, can be requested by that attorney. One linguist reports taking in any notes she needs on small cards and having multiple copies ready if asked. Judges appreciate any effort that helps move the action along.

THE WRAP-UP QUESTION

After you've gone through the points in your direct exam, your attorney will ask a final question that is intended to put a cap on everything you've said to that point. Most of the time, this question is pretty obvious. It is the same one you answered at the beginning and end of your deposition. It is the core point of all the work you've done on the case. If this is how it goes, well and good. But beware of the attorney who wants to stretch you a bit further, especially if it comes too close to the ultimate issue that is the province of the jury to decide—such as the guilt or innocence of the defendant. A few attorneys, especially in criminal cases, may try to do this, perhaps in spite of their better judgment. Their desire to win sometimes overcomes them. It's up to the expert witness to ward it off. Doing so also reinforces to the judge and jury that you know the limits of your role.

9

Cross-Examination Testimony

ONCE THE DIRECT EXAMINATION IS OVER, THE CROSS-examination begins. This may turn out to be on the following day. There are two schools of thought about the advantages of having the direct and cross-examinations occur continuously on the same day. One advantage to the witness, when these take place seamlessly, is that the opposing attorney has less time to think up new questions. On the other hand, it's often a relief to get an overnight break between the direct and cross, so that witnesses can find time to relax and collect their thoughts a bit. There are obvious advantages and disadvantages to both sequences. Judges are more sympathetic to the stress of jurors than to the comfort of witnesses, so it is more than likely that the judge will want to move the trial along quickly, and the cross will take place immediately. When it does, you can expect a brief recess before it begins. This means that you need to depend on the effectiveness of your previous preparation for both the direct and cross.

RECYCLING THE DEPOSITION

The attorney crossing you may begin with questions that were
asked of you in your deposition, which by now you should
be prepared to answer even better. Alternatively, the cross-
examination may begin with specific questions about your
direct exam. Your charts may be brought out again and challenged for their accuracy or the methods you used. You may
be asked why you didn't analyze materials that the opposing
lawyer considers more important than the ones you selected.

LUPA AGAIN

Unlike open-ended questions of the direct exam, the cross-
exam contains mostly yes/no and wh- questions. There is
no reason to look directly at the cross-examiner when these
questions are asked. Other than in responses to short answer
questions, it is sometimes wise to look at the jury when you
answer. Also unlike the direct exam, the cross-exam questions are often leading or suggestive. You should not be upset
by this, because it is well within the attorney's province to
do so. But for all questions, including tricky ones, the LUPA
advice noted in chapter 7 is good to follow: Listen, Understand, Pause, Answer.

All of the warnings mentioned in the previous section on
the deposition should be heeded. Don't volunteer anything,

because this can lead to a new line of questions that you don't need. Answer only the questions asked, nothing more, nothing less. Listen to the question before answering, repeating it if this seems helpful. Understand the question first. Pause long enough to allow for an objection. Answer truthfully, even if it seems to hurt. Say "I don't know" if you don't know. Don't guess. Watch out for vagueness or ambiguity in the questions as well as any presuppositions hidden in dependent clauses.

DIFFICULT QUESTIONS

Well-prepared expert witnesses have little to fear about questions that deal with the analysis they make. The devil is in the details. Certain kinds of questions may be more difficult to handle, the worst of which are hypothetical questions such as the one in this civil case.

Q: Suppose for a minute that the writer of this business proposal had seen the cost-pricing estimates produced by government accountants. Would the defendants then have been more accurate in the budget they submitted?

Answering such a question with "yes," "no," or "I suppose so" can lead to trouble. For one thing, you may have no idea what the lawyer is talking about. For all you know, the cost-pricing estimates he spoke of may never have actually existed.

And even if they did exist, you have no idea how their existence may have influenced the defendant's use of them in the proposal. It is good to be prepared for such hypothetical questions with responses such as the following.

A: I would need to speculate to answer your question.

Even better, you could say:

A: I'd like to answer this question, but to do so would require me to guess about something that I'm not qualified to guess about.

If the attorney you work with objects to the question, the judge may rule that you don't have to answer it. Expert witnesses are not supposed to speculate or make guesses. The judge knows this. So does the lawyer asking the question. The exchange is intended to trap you into going outside your expertise so that your other testimony can be impeached.

Hypothetical questions also can be couched in other less obvious ways, such as the following.

Q: Isn't it likely that the defendant could have heard the undercover agent say, "I got the woman dead for you?"

In this criminal case, the linguist had already testified that the video tape showed that when the agent said these words, the defendant had gotten out of the car and was walking to the trunk to get his sunglasses. His testimony was that at that point, both men were talking at the same time and, citing the taped discourse, the linguist had already shown that the defendant clearly continued talking about the benign topic that he had introduced before he got out of the car.

Again, answering such a question with "yes," "no," or "I suppose so" is dangerous. The linguist didn't really know how far away from each other the two men would have to be to actually still be able to hear each other. Furthermore, hearing does not mean paying attention or even processing what was said. The agent, now alone in the car, appeared to be talking into his hidden mike, taking advantage of the fact that the defendant would probably not hear it or attend to it when the agent said the bad stuff on the tape. The lawyer's question was intended to cast doubt on this testimony. So this hypothetical question was answered as follows.

A: The tape speaks for itself. It shows that the defendant was outside of the car, continuing to talk about the same topic that he introduced while he was still in the front seat. His voice is considerably harder to hear, however, because he was at a distance from the agent's hidden mike. Even if his ears were capable of hearing what the agent said, he gave no indication of paying any attention to it. He gave no response to it and he kept on talking about his own topic, both of which are consistent with not hearing what the agent said. The agent's words simply did not appear to register with him.

This answer is an example of how to take the hypothetical question and convert lemons into lemonade. It gave the witness a chance to repeat the major points that he had made in his previous testimony (repetition of good points is always desirable in testimony). It did not venture outside the expert's area of expertise, as it remains firmly based on his discourse analysis of the conversation. It does not say that the defendant did not hear the agent's words, for nobody can say this for sure, but it warded off the lawyer's inference about what happened.

Another question is one that can be more a surprise than difficult to answer. Academics aren't accustomed to being asked how much they are paid, but it is common in U.S. cross-examinations (but uncommon in the United Kingdom) to be asked, "How much are you getting paid for your testimony?" The way this question is asked can make it look to the jury as though you're being paid to shape your testimony to help your client. You need to think LUPA again here. Listen to the question first of all. You are not being paid for your testimony. You are being paid for the time you've spent working on your analysis and for the expertise you bring to the case. So your response should include this point, perhaps adding, "But I'm not being paid for my testimony." In the United States you may have to say how much you have been paid to date as well. Sometimes you'll be asked how much you charge per hour. Be totally honest here, but don't go into detail unless specifically asked for the exact number of hours or total you've earned. If asked, answer fully. Other experts are also paid, and it is often the case that their rates are even higher than yours. Refusing to answer this question, fudging it, or saying that you can't recall will look very bad.

TAKING BREAKS

In most U.S. trials the judge calls for ten- to fifteen-minute breaks after an hour and a half or so, mostly out of concern for the jury. But there is no hard-and-fast rule about this, and some judges tolerate longer work periods than others. If you have been on the witness stand a long time and feel the need for a bathroom break, it is perfectly within your rights to ask the judge for a brief recess. The judge then is likely to ask whichever lawyer is examining you how long this line of questioning is likely to last, leaving it to that attorney to decide when to take a break. It is unusual for that attorney to insist that a break is unnecessary or try to put it off for a long time. Attorneys need breaks, too, as do judges and juries. Although the judge may announce a ten-minute recess, it is common for it to last a few minutes longer. It is wise for you to be ready to return to the witness stand at the announced time, however, because it can be embarrassing for everyone else to be ready to resume while you are still missing.

During the break, you should not get into conversations with anyone, including your own lawyer. The bathroom is the place where you must be most vigilant about this because it is possible that it will be visited by attorneys and their associates from both sides. Even the slightest conversation between you and the attorney will often lead to the first question after the break, "Did you converse with your attorney during the break?" For the same reason, you should not converse with the opposing attorney, who may ask you to clarify something. Simply say, "I am not supposed to talk with anyone during the recess."

WHEN THE CROSS-EXAMINATION ENDS

When your cross-examination ends, the judge will thank you for your testimony and tell you that you can step down, to which a polite, "Thank you, your honor," is appropriate. But if the cross-examiner brought up something that your side's attorney wants to explore further, he or she may request a redirect, which is permitted only on topics that the cross-examiner has raised. A redirect is usually done to rehabilitate something that your attorney felt had not gone as planned or for which the jury may have gotten the wrong impression. This is usually a very brief event. If the cross-examiner is still not satisfied, he or she can ask to recross, again only on the topic that was discussed in the redirect. This exchange of recross and redirect could go on and on, but it usually doesn't.

WHEN THERE IS NO CROSS-EXAMINATION

In some criminal cases in which I've testified, there has been no cross-examination at all. I was puzzled by this until I learned that there are at least three reasons this happens. One is that the lawyer on the other side wants to give the jury the impression that the testimony was not worth much, not even enough to bother to cross-examine me. Another reason is that the attorney suspects that the testimony was powerful and doesn't want to emphasize it any more with further questions about it. A third reason to ignore crossing is that the lawyer is totally unprepared for it and doesn't have a clue about what to ask. Lawyers tend to avoid asking questions for which they don't know the answers. Doing so could come back to bite them.

In civil cases, however, you can fully expect to be cross-examined. As a rule, the cross experience is not nearly as uncomfortable as the deposition. Badgering and insulting are not common, largely because doing this makes a bad impression on jurors and judges. The judge polices the cross-examination for such incivility. Decorum is usually in abundance. When the judge finally dismisses you, usually saying only, "You may step down now," it is a good idea to thank the judge, get up, and walk confidently out of the courtroom saying nothing to anyone.

WHEN THERE IS AN OPPOSING LINGUIST

In many civil cases in the United States, a linguist is hired by both sides. This practice appears to be growing in the United Kingdom as well, although it is still rather rare there. As our discipline becomes better known, more attorneys are turning to linguists to help with civil disputes in particular but

also in some criminal cases. In a procedure relatively unknown in the United States, judges in the United Kingdom
sometimes ask the opposing linguist witnesses to get together
and produce an agreed statement. When a linguist appears
in opposition to your analysis and testimony, it can lead to
some interesting and awkward situations.

Linguists are trained to argue and even disagree with each
other's analysis. That's how progress is made in our field.
Unfortunately, the courtroom is a place where reasonable
disagreements carry very different weight. The focus of a law
case is on winning, not on developing our field. For this reason, someone's analysis and argument has to win, at least in
the minds of the judge and jury. It is sometimes the case that
the linguist on the other side of the case has better language
data to work with in the first place (this has happened to me).
There is no reasonable way to overcome such a handicap.
Linguist expert witnesses can only make their honest and best
possible case with the resources given them. If the other side's
case prevails, it is not necessarily a defeat. Experts are expected to do the best they can without distorting the evidence.
If their side loses the case, it's not necessarily the linguist's
fault.

First, once it is made known to you who the opposing linguist is, you are not to speak with that person about the case.
If you are colleagues or friends, as is often the case, even your
casual conversations get shortened and tense. Having shared
your field and experiences with that person in the past, suddenly you find yourself awkwardly avoiding the subject of

this case. I've had this experience several times now, and I can say that it is a great relief when the trial is over.

NOT ADVERSARIES

Because opposing lawyers play the role of adversaries during the case, it seems natural that you, a linguistics expert, will also be an adversary to the other side's linguistics expert. This, of course, is nonsense, especially when the two of you are colleagues and friends. In one case when the other side announced that it was also using a linguist, it turns out that I had actually written recommendations for his promotion and tenure as well as a very positive review of one of his manuscripts for a publisher. We had known each other for many years and were, to say the least, on the friendliest of terms. In this civil case, the lawyers decided that each linguist would sit in on the other's deposition, apparently to consult with the attorneys we worked with and advise them while they deposed each of us separately. One of the first questions asked of my opponent was whether he knew me. He responded happily that he did, mentioning the favors I had done him in his career. When it came my turn to be deposed, I mentioned that my opponent had written one of my favorite books in the area. It's hard to know exactly what the lawyers thought about our exchange of compliments and pleasantries, but it was clearly not what they had expected. Law cases are often about impeaching qualifications of the witnesses, but in this one they had a rather difficult time accomplishing this.

I relate this story to point out the need for experts to keep from joining in with their own attorneys in becoming an advocate rather than being a proper, objective expert. Our task is to present our analyses, no matter what the analysis of the opposing linguist might be. My friend and I actually agreed on many points and disagreed on a few as well. The disagreements were about our particular ways of analyzing the text placed before us. Linguists do this all the time, and the tension of being on opposite sides in a law case shouldn't change this.

This story contrasts sharply with my experience of having an opposing linguist in a different case. We knew of each other but didn't really have much contact in our professional careers. Oddly enough, the other linguist expressed no disagreement with the conclusions of my analysis but testified that the field of linguistics, as he defined it, could not have led me to such conclusions. This was a case of "my brand of linguistics is better than yours." It's hard to know what the judge in this bench trial made of this disagreement, because he couldn't care much about the internal squabbles in our field. I suspect that this case illustrates how competing expert witnesses should not behave in the forensic context. Even if the other linguist had established his superiority over my brand of linguistics, his testimony did little to help his side of the case. It may have been an interesting discussion for a linguistics meeting, but it had no useful place in this event.

WHEN OTHER LINGUISTS OBSERVE YOU

It is only natural that linguists who work in law cases may be interested in observing other linguists testifying at trial. Much can be learned this way, and it is a practice to be advocated. But when a linguist is testifying and looks out at the audience in the courtroom and spots another linguist observing the procedure, it can be a bit disconcerting. Experts have to communicate what they know to a jury who doesn't have the same knowledge or background. To do this requires using terminology that the jury knows, gently leading them to understand the complexities of linguistic analysis without really knowing it. In short, it can look like dumbing down to another linguist who happens to be observing.

I had such an experience when I was testifying in a money laundering case. I was sailing along through my testimony when I looked out and saw a local linguist sitting in the audience. I didn't know him well, but I knew that his training was more recent than my own, and I feared that I might be saying something that would cause him to think that I was less than accurate in my analytical procedures. As it turned out, this wasn't at all true, but it affected me just the same. Fortunately for me, the sinking feeling passed quickly, and I finished what I had to say effectively enough to help the client be acquitted. There needs to be a shared understanding among forensic linguists that we can't say everything we know at trial and that we can't be as technical or complete as we are when we address our fellow linguists only.

Linguistic experts who see other linguists observing them can perhaps take comfort in the fact that we all adjust our speech toward our audiences. Physicians who use medical school language when trying to explain symptoms and procedures may impress patients greatly with their erudition, but in the end, these doctors are not very likely to be understood. And what good would a similar erudition do linguists when they try to teach jurors in the courtroom? It is much better to establish solidarity and even intimacy with the jury rather than to allow technical language to create a distance between expert and juror.

10

Ethical Issues

LINGUISTS DON'T NEED TO BE REMINDED THAT FORENSIC consultants have certain ethical responsibilities. We can't work for both sides in a given case, for example, and we must tell the truth at all times. Such things are obvious, but some other ethical issues may be raised as well.

The first ethical issue to face is whether you are truly qualified to take on the case. You should be well trained in the areas of linguistics required for the analysis you'll present. For example, voice identification cases may require the knowledge of acoustic phonetics and the ability to use the electronic equipment needed. A specialization in Old English may be great for the university, but it hardly qualifies as expertise for a trademark case. What's worse, the opposing side can hire an expert with the appropriate training to attack such an analysis. It's better to know your limits and stay within them. It's an ethical responsibility to the attorney and yourself.

Some linguists find it problematic to agree to work on a case that has some morally undesirable aspects to it. For

example, working with the criminal attorney who is defend-
ing a person accused of soliciting murder or with a civil lawyer whose client is accused of harming the environment may
pose an ethical dilemma that may seem hard to overcome.
Some linguists may have their own moral reasons to simply
avoid such cases altogether. But working on a case does not
mean that you have to agree with or support the accusations
or positions of the clients on either side. The law permits the
expression of two sides of any dispute, and lawyers are hired
to represent such positions and their clients involved in them.
In contrast, linguistic consultants are not advocates for either
side. We simply analyze the evidence and present it. We may
not like the clients, the lawyers, or the charges, but such feelings should matter little in how we do our work, which is
outside the area of the ultimate outcome of the case. There is
no ethical problem in analyzing such data unless we join in
the advocacy, distort the data, or do not carry out the most
complete and accurate analysis possible.

Obviously, experts should always do the best work they
are able to provide. When we are shown to be wrong, we
should admit it as gracefully as possible and adjust our analysis. This will not always ruin the lawyer's case. Excuses or,
worse yet, cover-ups almost always lead to disaster. Sometimes, especially when on the witness stand or in depositions,
admitting an error actually can be helpful. Judges and juries
appreciate expertise, not infallibility.

If the case you work on has some downsides, the attorney
may wish to skirt them in your testimony. Suppose your analy-

sis has both positive and negative implications for the client. Although it may seem like an ethical issue not to present the negative aspects in your testimony, this is not really your problem. It's up to the lawyers on the other side to bring them out, if indeed they even figure them out. If they do figure them out and ask you about them, all you can do is agree that these facts exist. They probably won't ask you why you ignored them, but if they do, all you can say is that you weren't asked about them in your direct examination.

Things can get a bit dicey when the client's lawyer doesn't give you all the information you need, especially when these data might damage the case. If this is brought up by the opposing attorney, all you can say is that you were never given that data to analyze. This becomes the attorney's problem to explain, not yours.

Perhaps the greatest challenge to ethical objectivity can come from the relationship you may develop with the client's lawyers. As mentioned earlier, they are, by definition, an advocacy team, and it's often much too easy to join with them in this. Resist this temptation. The linguist has no responsibility to become an advocate for the client. Our only responsibility is to analyze the data in the case as objectively as possible. One way to control this is to be certain that the analysis you do would be exactly the same if your were doing it for the opposing side. The ultimate decisions in the case, whether civil or criminal, are always left to those who must weigh the facts—the jury or, in bench trials, the judge. The expert should never be asked to reach those decisions. If the

client's attorney pushes you uncomfortably close to that position, the best thing to say is that it's not your role. It's the
responsibility of the trier of the evidence. Oddly enough,
saying this tends to endear the witness to the jury and judge.

Related to the ethical issue of joining the lawyer's team as
an advocate is the temptation to discredit the opposing linguist
in a case. It is perfectly appropriate to disagree with that
linguist's analysis, but one should avoid the temptation to try
to impeach that linguist with *ad hominem* arguments. This
surely gives the appearance of advocacy and, in any case, it
usually does not play well with judges and juries.

Even telling the truth can be uncomfortable on occasion.
There may be times when you really don't know the answer
to a question or you may have forgotten something you once
knew. When this happens, it's best to admit it truthfully. This
little error is unlikely to do much damage anyway, because
jurors can identify with the human plight of forgetting things
once in a while, especially in the context of a high-stress trial.
It can be far worse to try to bluff your way through such
questions.

There are two types of work that linguists can do in law
cases: consult and advise lawyers about your analysis, and
testify in court. It is rare, however, that attorneys will call you
originally only to consult on a case. At that point, their ex-
pectation is usually that a trial will take place, and they don't
want to preclude the possibility of your serving as an expert
witness sometime down the road. If you prefer not to testify
in a case, it is only fair to advise attorneys about this at the

very beginning of your relationship. Failure to reveal this or changing your mind about it after agreeing to do so is unfair to the attorney and is highly unethical practice.

When it appears that your ongoing analysis does not support the case of the lawyers you're working with, it is also ethical practice to make this clear to them as early as possible. Although this often ends your relationship, in most cases your findings will be very useful information for them to keep in mind as they work toward settlement in civil cases or toward plea bargains in criminal actions. Lawyers need realistic assistance, not sugarcoating that might actually lead them to disastrous results.

A relatively rare ethical dilemma can occur when after you've already agreed to work with the attorney on one side of a case, the lawyer for the other side calls you to be an expert on that side. What should you tell the second lawyer? Obviously, you can't agree to work for both sides, but do you have to tell the second lawyer exactly why? Sometimes not. When the witness lists have not yet been submitted, it's best to politely decline the second attorney's request without explanation. Revealing your presence on the court's witness list can become a problem for the attorney with whom you've already agreed to work. The truth will come out soon enough, and you haven't let any cats out of the bag too early.

When you know the linguist engaged by the opposing side in a case, it's best to cease contact with that person until the case is settled. I describe one such experience in my book *Linguistics Battles in Trademark Disputes* (2002). A good friend was my opposition. We had been communicating with each other about many things up to that point, but we carefully avoided each other until the case ended. Even when we were in the same city at the time of the trial and had three days of downtime waiting to testify, we preserved our distance and silence. It's better to avoid even the very appearance of a potential ethics problem.

It's normal when a lawyer calls to request the linguist's services that payment for work can be expected. That's what *consulting* means. In some cases, however, linguists and other consultants are asked to work pro bono, and sometimes they even volunteer to do this. Lawyers take a certain amount of cases on a pro bono basis, and linguists might be expected to do the same, especially in cases involving indigent people or nonprofit groups. One ethical rule of thumb is that if the lawyer works pro bono, the linguist might consider doing the same.

It has been suggested that there also may be ethical issues involved in the way linguists write or speak about cases once they are resolved. For example, one linguist has observed that when academic research is supported by someone with a financial stake in the outcome, it is always appropriate to acknowledge such support in speeches or writings. By analogy, it is suggested that linguists should always report whether they are paid for work in law cases. Other linguists find this notion strange, because it is only to be expected that people, including academics, will be paid for their time, effort and products in any type of consulting work, including forensic linguistics. They argue that in most civil cases, such as trademark infringement, product liability, and contract disputes, the outcome virtually always has a financial stake, making this the expected situation. The unsettled quandary here seems to be whether support for research from the National Science Foundation or other sources is the same as work paid for consulting in general or forensic work in particular. An additional issue arises when however noble and right it may be to work without pay in some cases, calling attention to this tends to give the appearance of bragging about one's generosity and virtue. The ethical concern about reporting whether payment is made for services has not been adequately resolved at this point in time.

Forensic linguists who hold university appointments may have an ethical issue about the amount of money earned and time spent on consulting. They should be sure to follow the requirements of their university contract in such matters. Such contracts often indicate the percentage of time permissible on outside consulting projects, at least during the period of work when teaching is done. Complicating this is that when linguists are teaching courses involving forensic linguistic issues, the cases they work on actually contribute data and examples to their courses in the same way that other funded research projects do. Openness is the safest way to go in this rather murky ethical issue.

11

Using Your Experience
to Write Articles or Books

I HAVE POINTED OUT THAT EXPERTS NEED TO HAVE PUB-
lications that support their linguistic expertise in their field.
Once you've used linguistics to help with law cases, it can be
useful to transform your experiences to articles or books. Expertise in linguistics will make you acceptable as an expert
witness, and experience in actual law cases will open the
door of acceptability even wider. An opposing attorney would
have great difficulty complaining that you have no experience in the legal arena and therefore that you don't belong
in a trial. Even a few cases that you can cite will usually
make such a complaint difficult. And when you can cite
articles or books that you've published relating linguistics
to law cases, objections to your expertise are even more difficult to make.

In the United States, once the case is settled and over, there
are no restrictions on using data from a law case in your books
or articles (unless the expert has signed a confidentiality agreement with the case attorney that restricts such activity). Otherwise the material is considered to be in the public domain. In

the United Kingdom, however, stronger restrictions exist, including the need to get explicit permission in writing if you are to use such materials.

The only downside to publishing is that what you write becomes available for opposing lawyers to study and sometimes they will try to use it against you. I have had this happen several times, but it turned out to have no real disadvantage for me. The amount of time and effort it takes an opposing lawyer to read and assimilate what you've written usually discourages them. When they do managed to frame what they think is a challenging question, it is usually quite easy to answer it. In my experience, more often than not when the lawyer carries my books or articles into the courtroom, it's done more as a perceived threat to me than to actually discredit my testimony.

As a relatively new area of work, forensic linguistics is fairly wide open to approaches that apply linguistics to specific types of cases. For example, I have published books describing how speech acts can be applied to criminal cases (Shuy 1993), on how linguistics applies to police interrogation and confession cases (Shuy 1998b), on ways of dealing with convoluted government prose (Shuy 1998a), how linguistic analysis works in trademark cases (Shuy 2002), and on conversational strategies used by undercover law enforcement officers (Shuy 2005). This is only a small segment of this fruitful area of publishing. Other similar types of books are listed in chapter 13. Each case you work on offers interesting and sometimes unique data for which linguistic insights can be helpful. Sometimes the data can even suggest new insights about how language works.

Book publishers are gradually becoming interested in getting forensic linguistics books into print. Oxford University Press, The University of Chicago Press, Palgrave Macmillan, Blackwell, Georgetown University Press, Routledge, Continuum, Peter Lang, Elsevier, and CRC Press have become active in this area in recent years. I expect others to follow soon.

You can also publish academic articles, of course, especially in the journals *Speech Language and the Law*; *Language and Society*; *Language, Discourse and Society*, *Text*; *Discourse Processes*; *American Speech*; and others.

A good way to test the potential of a publishable book or article is first to give a presentation on it at academic meetings such as the International Association of Forensic Linguists, the Linguistic Society of America, the American Dialect Society, the American Association of Applied Linguistics, the International Pragmatics Association, and many others. Conference papers beget journal articles, and clusters of journal articles on the same theme beget books. The more your curriculum vitae displays peer-reviewed and accepted articles on forensic linguistics, the more you are considered an expert forensic linguist.

If you decide that you might want to use the cases you've worked on for articles or books, it is important that you keep complete files of these cases so that you'll have them when at some future date you decide to write about them. Save everything you're permitted to keep: tapes, indictments, depositions, police reports, suicide notes, advertisements, regulations, business contracts, and even newspaper reports of the trials. These should be marked in ways that you can easily identify them, even years later. I file my own cases in banker boxes with labels indicating type of case (i.e., bribery, money laundering, contract dispute, product liability, trademark, age discrimination, perjury, etc.), along with the date, lawyer's name, and sometimes even the client's name when it is a high-profile case. This obviously requires lots of storage space in your basement or garage. One odd effect of my keeping such files is that sometimes months or even years later the client or the lawyer will call me for copies of some data or aspect of the case. Apparently attorneys are not always good repositories of their completed cases. More than once I've been asked to supply materials that attorneys have misplaced or lost.

REFERENCES
Shuy, Roger W. 1993. *Language Crimes.* Oxford: Blackwell.
Shuy, Roger W. 1998a. *Bureaucratic Language in Government and Business.* Washington, DC: Georgetown University Press.
Shuy, Roger W. 1998b. *The Language of Confession, Interrogation and Deception.* Thousand Oaks, CA: Sage.
Shuy, Roger W. 2002. *Linguistic Battles in Trademark Disputes.* Houndmills, U.K.: Palgrave Macmillan.
Shuy, Roger W. 2005. *Creating Language Crimes: How Law Enforcement Uses and Misuses Language.* New York: Oxford University Press.

12

Using Your Experience to Teach Courses

As MENTIONED EARLIER, THERE SEEMS TO BE A GROWING tendency to teach college courses in various aspects of forensic linguistics. Although this may have certain benefits, I consider the major advantages for teaching to be the rich examples that law cases can provide to core linguistics courses, such as phonetics, morphology, syntax, semantics, pragmatics, speech acts, discourse analysis, sociolinguistics, lexicography, and language assessment. The examples taken from real-life contexts can stimulate student interest in ways that conventional made-up sentences often cannot. Data about the reality of bribes, solicitation to murder, confession statements, and other criminal case data can generate considerable excitement among today's students, who have been brought up on television programs that regularly deal with solving crimes. Civil case topics of discrimination by age, gender, race, and employment; contract disputes; hazard statements on products; deceptive trade practices; and copyright disputes can provide stimulating revelations about how language works in the real world of commerce.

Colleges and universities that are not afraid to reach out across conventional disciplinary lines may take advantage of the fact that forensic linguistic work is closely related to programs in criminology, business, psychology, sociology, and, of course, law. Many forensic linguists today have managed such cross-disciplinary relationships. For example, even in my retirement I regularly serve as an expert witness at sample trials at the local university's law school classes, where law students are learning the art of direct and cross-examination. I've also given lectures at the law school on different topics relating linguistics to law. Other senior linguists have been forging relationships with law schools and other related departments. Business majors would do well to know more about the importance of language in contract negotiations and disputes, how money launderers are captured in undercover tape-recorded conversations, and how texts can be compared in copyright cases. The field of forensic linguistics has only begun to flex its cross-disciplinary muscles in college and university settings.

13

Some Useful Books for the Forensic Linguist's Library

FORENSIC LINGUISTICS IS STILL A RELATIVELY NEW FIELD, and therefore, it is still reasonably easy to absorb the majority of its literature. The following categorizes the major, relatively recent books available at the time of this writing. Forensic linguists should probably own these books and use them as handy references in their personal libraries. This list does not include the valuable and relevant journal articles or chapters in collected works in the field of linguistics, psychology, sociology, or other disciplines. For such, refer to the comprehensive (but now a bit outdated) bibliography by Judith Levi. Other important, available resources include the forensic linguistics e-mail discussion list, forensiclinguistics@jiscmail .ac.uk, and the indispensable *International Journal of Speech, Language and the Law,* the publication of the International Association of Forensic Linguistics.

BIBLIOGRAPHY OF FORENSIC LINGUISTICS
Levi, Judith N. 1994. *Language and Law: A Bibliographic Guide to Social Science Research in the U.S.A.* Teaching Resource Bulletin No. 4. Chicago: American Bar Association.

INTRODUCTIONS TO FORENSIC LINGUISTICS

Gibbons, John. 2003. *Forensic Linguistics: An Introduction to the Language in the Justice System.* Oxford: Blackwell.

McMenamin, Gerald. 2002. *Forensic Linguistics: Advances in Forensic Stylistics.* Boca Raton, FL: CRC Press.

Olsson, John. 2004. *Forensic Linguistics: An Introduction to Language, Crime and the Law.* London: Continuum.

EDITED COLLECTIONS OF FORENSIC LINGUISTIC WORK

Cotterill, Janet (ed.). 2002. *Language in the Legal Process.* Houndmills, U.K.: Palgrave Macmillan.

Eades, Diana (ed.). 1995. *Language in Evidence: Issues Confronting Aboriginal and Multicultural Australia.* Sydney: University of New South Wales Press.

Gibbons, John (ed.). 1994. *Language and the Law.* London: Longman.

Kniffka, Hannes (ed.). 1996. *Recent Developments in Forensic Linguistics.* Frankfurt: Peter Lang.

Levi, Judith N., and Anne Graffam Walker (eds.). 1990. *Language in the Judicial Process.* New York: Plenum Press.

Rieber, Robert, and William A. Stewart (eds.). 1990. *The Language Scientist as Expert in the Legal Setting: Issues in Forensic Linguistics.* New York: Annals of the New York Academy of Sciences, vol. 606.

LEGAL LANGUAGE

Conley, John M., and William M. O'Barr. 1990. *Rules versus Relationships: The Ethnography of Legal Discourse.* Chicago: University of Chicago Press.

Danet, Brenda. 1980. Language in the Legal Process. Special Issue of *The Law and Society Review.*

Kurzon, Dennis. 1986. *It Is Hereby Performed: Legal Speech Acts.* Amsterdam: John Benjamins.

Mellinkoff, David. 1963. *The Language of the Law.* Boston: Little Brown.

Tiersma, Peter. 1999. *Legal Language*. Chicago: University of Chicago Press.

TRIAL LANGUAGE

Conley, John M., and William A. O'Barr. 1998. *Just Words: Law, Language and Power*. Chicago: University of Chicago Press.

Cotterill, Janet. 2003. *Language and Power in Court: A Linguistic Analysis of the O.J. Simpson Trial*. Houndmills, U.K.: Palgrave Macmillan.

Lakoff, Robin Tolmach. 2000. *The Language War*. Berkeley: University of California Press.

Matoesian, Gregory M. 1993. *Reproducing Rape: Domination through Talk in the Courtroom*. Chicago: University of Chicago Press.

O'Barr, William M. 1982. *Linguistic Evidence: Language, Power, and Strategy in the Courtroom*. New York: Academic Press.

Stygall, Gail. 1994. *Trial Language: Differential Discourse Processing and Discursive Formation*. Amsterdam: John Benjamins.

THE LANGUAGE OF JUDGES

Philips, Susan U. 1998. *Ideology in the Language of Judges: How Judges Practice Law, Politics, and Courtroom Control*. New York: Oxford University Press.

Solan, Lawrence M. 1993. *The Language of Judges*. Chicago: University of Chicago Press.

LANGUAGE AND CRIMINAL LAW

Shuy, Roger W. 1993. *Language Crimes*. Oxford: Blackwell.

Shuy, Roger W. 1998. *The Language of Confession, Interrogation and Deception*. Thousand Oaks CA: Sage.

Shuy, Roger W. 2005. *Creating Language Crimes: How Law Enforcement Uses and Misuses Language*. New York: Oxford University Press.

Solan, Lawrence M., and Peter M. Tiersma. 2005. *Speaking of Crime: The Language of Criminal Justice*. Chicago: University of Chicago Press.

LANGUAGE AND CIVIL LAW

Cushing, Steven. 1994. *Fatal Words: Communication Clashes and Aircraft Crashes.* Chicago: University of Chicago Press.

Shuy, Roger W. 2002. *Linguistic Battles in Trademark Disputes.* Houndmills, U.K.: Palgrave Macmillan.

VOICE IDENTIFICATION

Baldwin, John, and Peter French. 1990. *Forensic Phonetics.* London: Pinter.

Hollien, Harry. 1990. *The Acoustics of Crime: The New Science of Forensic Phonetics.* New York: Plenum Press.

Tosi, Oscar. 1979. *Voice Indentification: Theory and Legal Applications.* Baltimore: University Park Press.

AUTHORSHIP IDENTIFICATION

McMenamin, Gerald R. 1993. *Forensic Stylistics.* Amsterdam: Elsevier.

Olsson, John. 2004. *Forensic Linguistics: An Introduction to Language, Crime and the Law.* London: Continuum.

GOVERNMENT LANGUAGE

Shuy, Roger W. 1998. *Bureaucratic Language in Government and Business.* Washington, DC: Georgetown University Press.

LANGUAGE OF MINORITIES

Berk-Seligson, Susan. 1990. *The Bilingual Courtroom: Court Interpreters in the Judicial Process.* Chicago: University of Chicago Press.

Chambers, John (ed.). 1983. *Black English: Educational Equity and the Law.* Ann Arbor, MI: Karoma.

Lucas, Ceil (ed.). 2003. *Language and the Law in Deaf Communities.* Washington, DC: Gallaudet University Press.

LANGUAGE AND DECEPTION

Galasinski, Dariusz. 2000. *The Language of Deception: A Discourse Analytical Study.* Thousand Oaks, CA: Sage.

Shuy, Roger W. 1998. *The Language of Confession, Interrogation and Deception.* Thousand Oaks, CA: Sage.

LANGUAGE IN CHILD SEX ABUSE CASES

Ceci, Stephen J., and Maggie Bruck. 1995. *Jeopardy in the Courtroom: A Scientific Analysis of Children's Testimony.* Washington, DC: American Psychological Association.

Walker, Anne Graffam. 1999. *Handbook on Questioning Children.* 2nd edition. Chicago: American Bar Association Center on Children and Law.

Index